Blessings
WE CELEBRATE

BLESSINGS
WE CELEBRATE
From Our House to Yours

JUNIOR LEAGUE OF HAMPTON ROADS, INC.

Hillsboro Press
PROVIDENCE PUBLISHING CORPORATION

**JUNIOR LEAGUE OF
HAMPTON ROADS, INC.**
Women building better communities

Printed in the United States of America

10   09   08   07   06   1   2   3   4   5

Library of Congress Control Number: 2006934597

ISBN-13: 978-1-57736-373-6
ISBN-10: 1-57736-373-6

Illustrations and *Seedling* cover illustration by Nancy Thomas
Cover design by Joey McNair
Page design by Joey McNair and LeAnna Massingille

Scripture verses marked GNT are taken from the Good News Translation—Second Edition, Copyright 1992 by American Bible Society. Used by Permission. Scripture verses marked KJV are taken from the Holy Bible, King James Version.

The Junior League of Hampton Roads, Inc. gratefully acknowledges all the individuals who submitted blessings for this project, and the authors and publishers who have generously granted permission for their materials to be used. If the source of a blessing is not noted, it is because the material is either in public domain or the original authorship could not be determined.

For additional copies of *Blessings We Celebrate*, contact the Junior League of Hampton Roads, Inc.
757-873-0281 • www.jlhr.org

Hillsboro Press

an imprint of
Providence Publishing Corporation
238 Seaboard Lane • Franklin, Tennessee 37067
www.providence-publishing.com
800-321-5692

From Our House to Yours,

a Personal Blessing

To:

From:

CONTENTS

ILLUSTRATIONS

PREFACE

A dynamic group of women got together for a planning meeting shortly after September 11, 2001. Since many in the group were members of the Junior League of Hampton Roads, they decided to create a new fundraising project that would both benefit the Junior League and be meaningful and lasting.

A member of the book committee mentioned that she had noticed that when her third child's friends came over during meal time, they did not seem comfortable sharing a blessing as did the friends of her older children. She thought it would be powerful to create a book of blessings that could be displayed on table tops and used on such occasions.

Thus began *Blessings We Celebrate*. The project began with asking people to share a part of their family traditions and childhood blessings with the committee. Collecting the blessings proved to be much more difficult than anticipated. Many people did not submit blessings because they felt their blessings would be well known. Others said that their blessings were impromptu, having been created on the spur of the moment to go with special occasions (christening, marriage, birthday, graduation, etc.), and thus were not written down.

When the project first began, the intent was to create a collection of blessings, but it became the sharing of people's lives in good times and bad. Collecting these blessings and stories was a wonderful experience and one that the committee will cherish for years to come. We hope that this book will be a special part of the life of your family and those that you care about. When you feel you need inspiration, open these pages. From our hearts to yours.

ACKNOWLEDGMENTS

The Junior League of Hampton Roads and the Blessings Book Committee wish to thank all persons who generously submitted blessings and stories for this book. Our appreciation goes to the Ad Hoc Book Committee members for their support and for sharing their time and talent: Amy Broad, Becky Tench, Betsy Miller, Candy Familant, Pam Minter, Kim Cross, Mary Johnson, Michelle Ferebee, Sally Sue Andrews, Shari-Ann Robertson, and Tyra Freed.

A special thanks to Sandy Donaldson, DeeDee Copeland, and Courtney Gardner, co-chairs of this project. Through their positive attitudes and steadfast dedication, they have become an inspiration to us all. To them, we say "THANKS!"

In addition, special thanks to Paul Garman, member of the Junior League of Hampton Roads Community Advisory Board, for his guidance in securing artistic resources for this book. Also, thank you to Chris Ambrosino of Nancy Thomas Galleries for his artistic talent and design skills. Thank you to Robyn Hylton Hansen, sustainer of the Junior League of Hampton Roads, for her legal guidance. And last but not least, a special thanks to Heather Walls of Ferguson Enterprises for keeping track of all submissions and correspondence over the years.

It is nice to see that spirit of voluntarism is alive and thriving in the Hampton Roads community. By working together, we can indeed change our community through our acts of kindness and caring.

Bon appetit

TABLE BLESSINGS

Well, Lord, a few minutes ago I was standing at the kitchen counter waiting for my bagel to toast and thinking how boring and ordinary the meal was . . . same old, same old. Every day I eat a bagel and drink juice and coffee for breakfast. Most days, my other meals don't vary much either.

I happened to glance at the front page of the newspaper and saw a photo of two African children holding bowls of what looked to me like paste. They had huge smiles on their faces. It struck me how extraordinary that bowl of whatever it was must have been to those kids who often go without anything to eat.

Thank you, Lord, for this feast and for all the other ways You will bless me today. Amen.

Nancy J. Jenkins

We're thankful for the many things
our heavenly Father sends:
for love and faith and strength and health,
for home and food and friends.
From *Table Graces: Prayers of Thanks*

—⁓—

Lord Jesus, Be Our Holy Guest
(*To be sung to the tune of* Tallis's Canon)
Lord Jesus, be our holy guest,
our morning joy, our evening rest;
and with our daily bread impart
Thy love and peace to every heart.
Henry J. van Dyke
From *Prayers from the Reformed Tradition*

—⁓—

Let us break bread together on our knees.
Let us break bread together on our knees.
When I fall on my knees with my face to the rising sun,
O Lord, have mercy on me.
African American Spiritual

—⁓—

Dear Lord, we thank You for this food.
Please make us helpful, kind, and good.

—⁓—

Dear Lord, watch over us throughout the day.
Be with us and guide us in work and in play.
And in all that we do and all that we say,
may we show Your love, in our own little way.
Mrs. L. C. "Ruby" Robertson Sr.

—⚡—

To those who hunger,
give bread.
And to us who have bread,
give the hunger for justice.
Latin American Prayer

—⚡—

Come, Lord Jesus,
be our guest,
and let Thy gifts
to us be blessed.
Martin Luther

—⚡—

God, we thank You for this food,
for rest and home and all things good,
for wind and rain and sun above,
but most of all for those we love.
Maryleona Frost

—⚡—

Do not throw upon the floor
a crumb you cannot eat,
for many a little hungry one
will think it quite a treat.
Mrs. L. C. "Ruby" Robertson Sr.

—⁂—

God bless this bunch as they munch their lunch!

—⁂—

Our Father, we give thanks to Thee for this food,
and we also remember in gratitude the men and women,
near and far, whose labors have made this meal possible.
Grant that they may enjoy the fruit of their labor without want,
And that they may be bound with us in a fellowship of thankful hearts.
From *Table Graces: Prayers of Thanks*

—⁂—

Thank You for food and shelter.
Thank You for family and friends.
Thank You for Your presence, Lord.
We count our blessings as we remember those
who are hungry and cold.
Bless them too, Father, and
guide us to share what we have.

—⁂—

4

Bless this food, O Lord,
and all who are gathered here.
Thank You for the abundance You provide.
Make us a blessing to You.

—⁂—

Thank You, Father God, for good and nourishing food.
Bless it to the health and building up of our bodies.

—⁂—

Thank You, Father, for bringing us together again.
Thank You for wonderful fellowship
and for letting us be hands and feet for You
as we serve others in Your name.
May our thoughts and words be pleasing to You.
In Jesus' name.

—⁂—

For this food, Lord, and for clean water we thank You.
Thank You for those who lovingly prepared this meal for our enjoyment.
Bless this food and bless those who prepared it and we who eat it.

—⁂—

If we have earned the right to eat this bread
happy indeed are we.
But if unmerited Thou give to us
may we more thankful be.
W. H. Neidlinger

—⁂—

For all our families and for friends,
for flowers and for food;
for life and laughter and for love,
we give Thee gratitude.

—⁂—

God is great, God is good.
Let us thank Him for our food.
By His hands, we all are fed.
Give us, Lord, our daily bread.
No book of blessings would be complete without this one,
which is often the first grace a child learns.

—⁂—

For food and all Thy gifts of love
we give Thee thanks and praise.
Look down, O Father, from above,
bless us all our days.

—⁓—

We thank Thee, Lord, for our daily bread
both for body and soul;
and do Thou keep us ever mindful
of Thy good providence;
through Jesus Christ our Lord.

—⁓—

We thank Thee, Lord, for happy hearts,
For rain and sunny weather.
We thank Thee, Lord, for this our food,
And that we are together.
Emilie Fendall Johnson

—⁓—

We give You thanks, O God, for this food
and for all Your many blessings.
Bless this meal to our use,
and us to Your loving and faithful service,
and make us always responsive
to the needs and rights of others.
For our Savior's sake.

—⁓—

BLESSINGS WE CELEBRATE

These busy days, we gather at Thy table, O Lord,
and recognize Thee as the giver of it all.
Transform this food into strength
and noble service for Christ's sake.

—◊◊◊—

Gracious Heavenly Father,
we thank Thee for food:
food for our bodies,
food for our minds,
and food for our spirits.
Help us appreciate these gifts
and use them in Thy service.

—◊◊◊—

Eternal Father, everlasting giver of good things,
we thank You for Your loving kindness to us.
In Your grace and will we are fed,
and in Your power and glory we are sustained.

—◊◊◊—

Great God, the giver of all good,
accept our praise and bless our food.
Grace, health, and strength to us afford,
through Jesus Christ, our blessed Lord.
Mennonite Grace

—◊◊◊—

Be present at our table, Lord,
be here and everywhere adored.
Thy creatures bless and grant that we
may feast in paradise with Thee.
John Cennick

—⪥—

Back of the bread is the flour.
Back of the flour is the mill.
And back of the mill
is the wind
and rain,
and the Father's will.
E. J. Allen-Williams

—⪥—

Dear Lord,
thank You for this food,
thank You for this day,
thank You for our family,
and we thank You for Your son, Jesus.
Adam Emory

—⪥—

Bless us, O Lord, and these Thy gifts
which we are about to receive
from Thy bounty, through Jesus Christ our Lord.
Amen.
Catholic Blessing

—⁄⁄⁄—

For every cup and plateful,
God make us truly grateful.

—⁄⁄⁄—

Thank You, God, for bestowing upon us Your love and grace.
We ask that You guide us to help others when in need.
We are grateful for our bounties.
May peace and love prevail, in Your name.
Lutheran Blessing

—⁄⁄⁄—

Doxology
Praise God, from whom all blessings flow;
praise Him all creatures here below;
praise Him above ye heavenly host;
praise Father, Son, and Holy Ghost.

—⁄⁄⁄—

Lord, make us truly thankful for this food, which we are about to
receive for nourishment and for the strengthening
of our bodies for Christ our Redeemer's sake.
Traditional African American Table Blessing

—⫘—

Lord God, we don't deserve the food before us today.
We don't deserve the salvation that is in Jesus Christ.
Through Your grace, we have both.
Bless the food to the nourishment of our bodies
and the hands that prepared it.
Michael Mappin

—⫘—

We thank Thee, Lord, for this our food;
God is love, God is love.
But more because of Jesus' blood;
God is love, God is love.
These mercies bless, and grant that we
may eat and drink, and live with Thee;
God is love, God is love.

—⫘—

BLESSINGS OF FAITH AND INSPIRATION

Here is an evening blessing, and a story of my love for my mother and of her precious journey home. When I was a child, my mother used to say a special blessing as she tucked me in bed each night. I had a four-poster twin bed and she would say this prayer:

Matthew, Mark, Luke, and John,
Bless the bed that I lay on.
Four corners to my bed;
Four angels around my head.
One to watch and one to pray,
And two to bear my soul away.

My mother lived a wonderful life. She had Alzheimer's during the last four years of her life, which was difficult, but it made her more like a child again. In her final days, she confused night and day time, and I stayed by her side.

She looked up one night and said, "They are happy. They are so happy up there. I want to go home." I said, "Mother, when Jesus comes for you, you just go to His arms."

continued . . .

The next night, she looked up from her bed and said, "He's coming. He is coming for me." Tears filled my eyes. I knew her time was near, but also I felt great joy for her life here on earth and her new life to come. That was the last thing she said.

The next day, Mother could not speak. I sat holding her hand and the prayer she always said for me came to my mind. "Mother, do you remember the blessing you said every night to me when you tucked me in bed? I want to say it for you," I said.

Matthew, Mark, Luke, and John,
Bless the bed that I lay on.
Four corners to my bed;
Four angels around my head.
One to watch and one to pray,
And two to bear my soul away.

Mother took her last breath just at the moment I finished the prayer. I closed her eyes and kissed her good-bye. I was so thankful to God that she had gone peacefully into Jesus' arms and the angels had borne her soul away.

I will treasure this blessing, which I said with my own children, and now hope to carry on this prayer with my granchildren, always thankfully remembering Mother's gentle journey home.
Rosemary Trible

━━〜〜━━

Dear God,
Let the light of Jesus shine through me
and let them not see me but see His love.
Mother Teresa

Break Thou the bread of life,
dear Lord, to me,
as Thou didst break the loaves
beside the sea.
Beyond the sacred page
I seek Thee, Lord;
my spirit pants for Thee,
O living Word!
Bless Thou the truth, dear Lord,
now unto me,
as Thou did bless the bread
by Galilee.
Then shall all bondage cease,
all fetter fall,
and I shall find my peace,
my all in all.
Mary A. Lathbury

—⁂—

Toast to the Now
Yesterday is history.
Tomorrow is a mystery.
Today is a gift.
And this is why
this moment is called the present.
Listen, look, taste, touch, and breathe the present.
Susan J. Erickson

—⁂—

May the Lord make your love for one
another and for all people grow more and more.
1 Thessalonians 3:12 (GNT)

—⚬—

A Moment to Pray
As the last ray of sunlight
paints the lovely day
in solitude, with thankfulness
I slowly kneel to pray.
Dear God, I ask with reverence
as daylight slowly fades,
what causes man his innocence
to lose before the grave?
If each of us like children
could laugh and dance and sing,
what beauty in our world we'd see
if each of us would bring
a smile, a hug, a word of cheer
to all we see and know,
so everyone within our reach
would seek Your love and grow.
For knowing You and loving You
brings all that we could ask.
Please now, my Lord, touch all of us
so in Your love we'll bask.
Gail S. Lentz
From *Hope for the Healing Heart*

—⚬—

The Prayer of St. Francis of Assisi

Lord, make me an instrument of Your peace.
Where there is hatred,
let me sow love;
where there is injury, pardon;
where there is doubt, faith;
where there is despair, hope;
where there is darkness, light;
and where there is sadness, joy.
O Divine Master, grant that I may not so much seek
to be consoled as to console;
to be understood, as to understand;
to be loved, as to love.
For it is in giving that we receive,
it is in pardoning that we are pardoned,
and it is in dying that we are born to eternal life.

—∿—

A Friar's Prayer

Lord, take me where You want me to go,
let me meet whom You want me to meet,
tell me what You want me to say,
and keep me out of Your way.
*Mychal F. Judge, a fifty-eight-year-old Franciscan and New York Fire Department
chaplain, was killed on September 11, 2001, at Ground Zero in Manhattan.
He had this prayer in his pocket; he carried it with him always.*

—∿—

A Thought from Marian Hornsby Bowditch, 1961
Be still
And know that He is there.
Be quiet
And know just when and where.

The twitter of a bird call,
The slamming of a door,
The bowing of a tree branch,
The way a plane can soar.

A squirrel on a nut hunt,
A child up in a tree,
A smile from a close friend,
A calming cup of tea.
The sharing of a funny joke,
The laughter that it brings,
The close companionship of Bill:
Not one, but many happy things.

It isn't just in praising hymns
And anguished concentration,
Open up your heart and mind
And live—in moderation.

It isn't shutting all else out,
But letting all things in
That gives you hope of understanding,
Compassion for other's sin.

It isn't such a "journey"
To seek this destination.
It's more a trip through happy times
And quiet observation.

It's the joy of opportunity
To have a heart that's light.
The Lord is on His heavenly throne
And there—just to your right.

Marian Hornsby Bowditch

*This blessing hung on Marian Hornsby Bowditch's kitchen wall since
she wrote it in 1961. When Marian died recently at the age of eighty-five,
one of her grandchildren read it at her funeral. It's a powerful blessing
to live by, full of wisdom and straight from the heart.*

———

O God, the giver of all good gifts,
we thank Thee for all the blessings which we have.
Give us always contented minds, cheerful hearts, and ready wills,
so that we may spend and be spent in the service of others,
after the example of Him who gave His life a ransom for many,
our Lord and Master, Jesus Christ.

From *Prayers for All Occasions*

———

BLESSINGS WE CELEBRATE

We praise Thee, O God, with gladness and humility
for all the joys of life.
For health and strength,
for the love of friends,
for work to do,
and play to re-create us.
We thank Thee for the adventure of life.
Above all, we thank Thee for Thy unspeakable gift
of Jesus Christ our Lord,
for the blessings that have come to us
through His body, the church.
And help us to show our thankfulness
not only with our lips, but in our lives,
always endeavoring to do that which shall please Thee;
through Jesus Christ our Lord.
From *Prayers for All Occasions*

—⁂—

Silence
God, I am waiting in Your silence.
Help me to rest in it, rather than become restless.
Teach me without words—Spirit to spirit.
Maybe You are quiet so that I must press in to hear.
I must learn to tune out the voices around me
and find the frequency of Your voice alone.
Perhaps You are not silent at all.
I am just not listening loud enough.
Judi Braddy

—⁂—

Tireless Guardian on our way,
Thou has kept us well this day.
While we thank Thee, we ask for Thy continued care,
for the forgiveness of our sins,
and for rest at the close of a busy day.
From the *Boy Scout Camp Chickahominy Interfaith Worship Service*

—⁓—

Kindness

Just a little act of kindness,
just a little word of cheer
help to make our living pleasant,
minimize both doubt and fear.
Jesus said, "Be meek and lowly,"
and He governs us with love,
just as God our heavenly Father
governs in the court above.
Jesus never hurt the feelings
of a person great or small.
Always He was kind and friendly;
we're assured He loves us all.
All the world is now in turmoil
caused by gross unfriendliness.
Peace will follow Christian living
by the watchword kindliness.

—⁓—

Bless the LORD, O my soul;
and all that is within me, bless his holy name.
Bless the LORD, O my soul, and forget not all his benefits;
who forgiveth all thine iniquities; who healeth all thy diseases;
who redeemeth thy life from destruction;
who crowneth thee with lovingkindness and tender mercies.
Psalm 103:1— 4 (KJV)

―᚜―

Dear God, when I am lonely,
and perhaps I feel despair,
let not my ailing heart forget
that You hear every prayer.
Remind me that no matter what
I do or fail to do,
there still is hope for me
as long as I have faith in You.
Let not my eyes be blinded
by some folly I commit,
but help me regret my wrong
and to make up for it.
Inspire me to put my fears
upon a hidden shelf, and in the future
never be sorry for myself.
Give me the restful sleep I need
before another dawn,
and bless me in the morning
with the courage to go on.

―᚜―

Invocation
2002 Annual Association of Junior Leagues International Conference

Sometime during this year to keep your heart in practice: May you do a secret good deed and not get caught at it. May you find a little island of time to read that book and write that letter and visit that lonely friend on the other side of town. May your next do-it-yourself project not look like you did it yourself. May all the predictions you've made for your firstborn's future come true. May just half of those optimistic predictions that your high school annual made for you come true. In a time of sink or swim, may you find you can walk to shore before you call the lifeguard. May you keep at least one ideal you can pass along to your kids. May you accidentally overhear someone saying something nice about you. If you run into an old school chum, may you both remember each other's names for introductions. May that lonely night be brightened by the telephone call that you've been waiting for. And when you trip and fall, may there be no one watching to laugh at you or feel sorry for you. Sometime soon may you be waved to by a celebrity, wagged at by a puppy, run to by a happy child, and counted on by someone you love. May what you see in the mirror delight you, and what others see in you delight them. May someone love you enough to forgive your faults, be blind to your blemishes, and tell the world about your virtues. May you live as God intended, in a world at peace and the awareness of God's love in every sunset, every flower's unfolding petals, every baby's smile, every lover's kiss, and every wonderful, astonishing, miraculous beat of your heart.

Karen Fetzer

—⁂—

You Are My Strength
If only I had trusted You, Lord,
with every little care.
If only I had realized
You are always there.
If only I had given You
the good things and the bad,
then, O my precious Lord, I know
I never would be sad.
For turning to Your loving arms
I'll find a hiding place,
and feel Your gentle spirit move
to shine upon my face.
Yes, in my darkest hour
You were always there for me.
I needed to reach out for You
and let not fear a bondage be.
The one who has the courage,
the one who stands against the wind
is fortified by God Himself
and turned from bitter sin.
So to my knees I'll go, Lord,
in good times and in bad
for only there can I become
fearless, faithful, glad!
Gail S. Lentz
From *Hope for the Healing Heart*

These Things I Ask For

I care not whether worldly wealth is mine,
nor if fame and fortune linger at my door.
Yearning for thrills is now all but forgotten,
as childhood fades these things alone I ask for:
laughter, for the world is bleak without it;
music, for my heart is full of song;
virtue, so I might walk with head erect;
strength, to help some weary soul along;
love, that my heart may e'er be tender;
comfort—I, too, have known grief's stinging lash;
honor, that my soul may not be tarnished;
judgment, to separate the pure from trash;
wisdom, better to cope with problems;
loyalty, to give my country aid;
endurance, for I know too well my weaknesses;
courage, to speak for justice unafraid;
observing eyes, to see the needs of others,
and to lend a hand, as on life's course they plod;
and last, but to me the most important,
the power of prayer, for I would talk with God.

—⁓—

The Synekdemos

Christ our God,
bless the food and drink of Your servants,
for You are holy always,
now and forever and to the ages of ages.
Daily prayer for Orthodox Christians

—⁓—

Daily Prayer for Orthodox Christians
We thank You, Christ our God,
for You have satisfied us with earthly gifts.
Do not deprive us of Your heavenly kingdom,
but as You, O Savior, came among Your disciples
and gave them peace,
come among us also and save us.

—⁂—

Grace
Permeate my thoughts, Lord,
bestow me grace I plead,
show me love and beauty,
fill my every need.
Lift the veil that keeps me
from Your throne today,
give me ears to hear You
and a voice to pray.
Let my spirit seek You,
wash my soul anew,
grant my travesties ransom
that I may see Your view.
Gail S. Lentz
From *Hope for the Healing Heart*

—⁂—

ABC newswoman and *Good Morning America* co-anchor Robin Roberts grew up in Pass Christian, Mississippi, and her family was familiar with storms, hurricanes, and other natural disasters. Still, nothing prepared them for Hurricane Katrina. With Katrina closing in, Robin's eighty-one-year-old mother, Lucimarian Tolliver Roberts, played the piano and prayed. Mrs. Roberts relied on her strong faith in God's favor, power, and protection as she stayed in her one-story home, even as Katrina churned toward the Gulf Coast on August 29, 2005, packing winds up to 145 mph. "God will take care of me," she thought. Mrs. Roberts later told the media, "I'll be fine right where I am. Wherever I am, God is. I felt that way, and said, We're not to be fearful." Robin was in New York while her mother and sisters were in Mississippi with Katrina bearing down on them. Even though Robin couldn't help her family evacuate or physically prepare for the devastating hurricane, she was able to help them in another way. She spoke with her mother by phone during the disaster and her mother requested Robin pray and bless her and the family members in the path of the storm. Robin prayed this prayer by James Dillet Freeman:

Prayer of Protection
The Light of God surrounds us.
The Love of God enfolds us.
The Power of God protects us, and
The Presence of God watches over us.
Wherever we are,
God is!
And all is well!
Amen.
Robin Roberts

As told in a speech during the 2006 National Conference on Volunteering and Service convened by the Points of Light Foundation and Volunteer National Network and the Corporation for National and Community Service; added details from the Presbyterian News Service.

NANCY THOMAS 2002

BLESSINGS FOR CHILDREN

A Little Ice Cream

Last week I took my children to a restaurant. My six-year-old asked if he could say grace. As we bowed our heads he said, "God is good. God is great. Thank you for the food, and I would even thank you more if Mom gets us ice cream for dessert. And liberty and justice for all! Amen!"

Along with the laughter from the other customers nearby, I heard a woman remark, "That's what's wrong with this country. Kids today don't even know how to pray. Asking God for ice cream! Why, I never!"

My son burst into tears and asked me, "Did I do it wrong? Is God mad at me?" As I held him and assured him that he had done a terrific job, and God was certainly not mad at him, an elderly gentleman approached the table. He winked at my son and said, "I happen to know that God thought that was a great prayer." Then in a theatrical whisper he added (indicating the woman whose remark had started this whole thing), "Too bad she never asks God for ice cream. A little ice cream is good for the soul sometimes."

Naturally, I bought my kids ice cream at the end of the meal. My son stared at his for a moment and then did something I will remember the rest of my life. He picked up his sundae and, without a word, walked over and placed it in front of the woman. With a big smile he told her, "Here, this is for you. Ice cream is good for the soul sometimes, and my soul is good already."

—◊—

A, B, C, D, E, F, G,
Thank You, God, for feeding me.
Mackenzie Gardner, age five

—⟋⟍—

Blessing for a Newborn
Tiny infant, expansive soul
guided by the hand of the Creator,
your life is a symbol of love realized.
Precious. Divine. Profound.
Blessed are we who have the privilege
of witnessing your days,
for surely your innocence and purity
are affirmation of life's goodness.
Sweet wonder, may your days be graced with peace
and may your heart be forever filled with joy.

—⟋⟍—

New Baby
The new baby, Lord, sits centerpiece proud on the dining table
as we eat a sleepy, still incredulous meal.
Where before there were only two at our table,
now there is a family eating together.
Only You, Creator, could come up with such a marvel,
and we are awed even in the midst of exhaustion and newness.
May our family dinner conversations, like the meals ahead,
nourish and fill as we continue the creating
You have begun, the making of a family.
Margaret Anne Huffman

God made the world so broad and grand
filled with blessings from His hand.
He made the sky so high and blue,
and all the little children, too.

—⚹—

Birthday Blessing

Though I'm only one year old
hear me as my hands I fold.
Thank You for the food I see
and the people close to me.
Bless the others far away
give them food by night and day.
Let me always grateful be
for blessings that you give to me.
*This is a birthday blessing that is changed each year to help
mark this special day in the life of a child. On the first birthday
the child is taught to fold his/her hands as Mom and Dad
recite the blessing. The child can say it independently in subsequent years.
"Now dear God, I'm two years old," etc.*

—⚹—

Heavenly Father,
thanks we say for the food we have today.
May there be enough to share
for all the children everywhere.

—⚹—

I thank You, God, for a hundred things . . .
the flowers that bloom,
the birds that sing.
The rain that drops,
the sun that shines,
ice cream and gum and lollipops!

—⚊—

Just Right

Not too big,
not too small,
not too short,
not too tall.
Some have green eyes,
some have brown.
Some live in the country,
some live in town.
In every one good and bad,
every one happy and sad,
no matter who you are or where,
I want you to know that I care.
In my sight
you're just right.
Jeff Adams

—⚊—

A Child's Grace
Thank You for the world so sweet,
thank You for the food we eat,
thank You for the birds that sing,
thank You, God, for everything.
Edith Rutter Leatham

—∞—

Bless us, Jesus, in our home;
and bless kids across the sea.
Please send needed food and drink
to children everywhere—and me.
From *Table Graces: Prayers of Thanks*

—∞—

Madeline's Blessing
We love our bread.
We love our butter.
But most of all we love each other.
Hayven Livers, first grader

—∞—

Thank You, God, for the beautiful day,
for home, for care, and for happy play.
Eleanor Weston Brown recalls that as children, "we recited this poem each night with our mother, Eleanor Weston Woodward. She knew it from a book of children's prayers and poems."

—∞—

God has created a new day,
silver and green and gold.
Live that the evening may find us
worthy His gifts to hold.
Lord, bless not only meat and drink,
but what we do and what we think.
So that in all our work and play,
we may grow better every day.
From *Table Graces: Prayers of Thanks*

—∿—

For bright lights and warm fires,
we thank Thee, O God.
For good food and the clothes we wear,
we thank Thee, O God.
For the love and care of mother and father,
we thank Thee, O God.
For friends who come to be our guests,
we thank Thee, O God.
For all things you have given us to enjoy,
we thank Thee, O God.
For true happiness which comes when we share,
we thank Thee, O God.
From *Table Graces: Prayers of Thanks*

—∿—

Prayer for a Child

Bless this milk and bless this bread,
bless this soft and waiting bed
where I presently shall be
wrapped in sweet security.
Through the darkness,
through the night,
my sleep till morning once again
beckons at the windowpane.
Bless the toys whose shapes I know,
the shoes that take me to and fro,
up and down and everywhere.
Bless my little painted chair.
Bless the lamplight, bless the fire,
bless the hands that never tire
in their loving care of me.
Bless my friends and family.
Bless my father and my mother
and keep us close to one another.
Bless the children far and near,
and keep them safe and free from fear.
So let me sleep and let me wake
in peace and health for Jesus' sake.
Rachel Field

Prayer for a Little Child
Dear Father in heaven,
I thank You for Jesus,
who came to bring us Your love,
and to teach us to love one another.
Help me to love everybody
and to do what He would like me to do.
Dear God, I thank You for all good things;
for my home, for food and clothing,
for my friends, for the flowers
and trees and birds—and everything;
and when I grow up help me to share
all my good things with others.
From *Prayers for All Occasions*

—⁂—

For fruit and milk,
for bread and meat,
for all this food, so good to eat—
we thank You, God.
From *Table Graces: Prayers of Thanks*

—⁂—

Johnny Appleseed
The Lord is good to me,
and so I thank the Lord
for giving me the things I need
the sun and the rain and the apple seed.
The Lord is good to me.
And every seed that grows
will grow into a tree,
and one day soon there'll be apples there,
for everyone in the world to share.
The Lord is good to me.
Oh, here I am 'neath the blue, blue sky
doing as I please.
Singing with my feathered friends
a song that seems to never end,
humming with the bees.
I wake up every day,
as happy as can be,
because I know that with His care
my apple trees, they will still be there.
The Lord's been good to me.

—⁓—

Thank You for our food and
Our friends and our family.
And help us to love each other. Amen.
Lee Summerell, age four

—⁓—

God Our Father
(Sung to the tune of "Frere Jacques")
God our Father, God our Father,
once again, once again,
we will sing our blessings
we will sing our blessings.
Amen, Amen.

―⁓―

Child's Blessings for All Hours
Morning
Father we thank You for the night
And for the pleasant morning light
For rest and food and loving care
And all that makes the world so fair.

Dinner
We bless You for the food we eat.
We bless You for the world so sweet,
For rest and food and loving care,
And all that makes the world so fair.

Night
Now I lay me down to sleep
I pray the Lord my soul to keep
If I die before I wake
I pray the Lord my soul to take.

―⁓―

Sometimes Blessings Come in Small Packages

Earlier this year my brother, two sisters, and I shared the agony of wondering whether my mother would make it though a serious illness. We had gone through similar experiences before and had found extraordinary strength in each other. We didn't cry or panic. Sometimes, however, what you need is not to be so strong but to allow yourself to feel the pain.

As I returned from a week at my mother's side in the hospital, I felt emotionally spent and broke into tears on the long ride home from the airport. Baffled, but not wanting to make things worse, my husband and grown son didn't know what to do except leave me alone as I had requested.

Sobbing alone in my room, I felt the gentle thump of my three-year-old grandson as he hopped on the foot of my bed.

"Grandma," he said, "what happened?

"Why are you crying?"

"I don't know," I said, as I held my stomach while lying in a fetal position.

"Let's pray," he said.

Surprised, I said through sobs, "What?"

"Let's pray," he repeated.

"Okay," I said.

He began with his eyes closed, "Dear Lord". . . and waiting for me to repeat after him, he said again, "Dear Lord . . ."

I repeated, "Dear Lord . . ."

"Heal this stomach," he said, as he slid his hands on my stomach.

"Heal this stomach," I repeated.

"Heal this leg," he said, as he touched my leg. "Heal this leg," I repeated.

"In Jesus' name," he said. I repeated, "In Jesus' name."

And as if he felt I needed to show more conviction, he said, "In Jesus' name." Likewise, I said, "In Jesus' name."

"Amen," he said and I echoed, "Amen."

As he opened his eyes, my little angel said, "Grandma, do you feel better, now?"

Now, with a smile instead of tears, I said, "Yes, I do, baby."

Laurine Press

As teenagers we come before Thee and give thanks
for the strength and awareness that comes each day
as we bridge the difficult journey from childhood to adulthood.
God sustains us in class and shares our joy.
As our minds and bodies grow may we be ever mindful
of the physical and spiritual nourishment
which God's presence provides.
Amen.
From *Table Graces: Prayers of Thanks*

—⁓—

Once a year, I become not just Aunt Linda, but also director of "Cousins Camp." Ten first cousins, ages eight to twenty-six, gather for a few days and nights of fun, games, and mostly just hanging out together. Meals are simple and kid-focused. The favorite meal is "MYOS"—Make Your Own Sandwich. The fixings are spread on the table and each person is allowed to put whatever they choose on their sandwich, no restrictions. One year, a six-year-old put just orange things on his sandwich—carrots, cheese, and barbecue potato chips. He cleaned his plate that meal! At each meal we sing our blessing to the tune of "Frere Jacques."

Thank You, God, thank You God,
For our food, for our food,
And all our cousins, and all our cousins,
Amen. Amen.
Linda Gilden

—⁓—

My husband and I had been teaching our three-year-old son Zachary to use a tissue when he sneezed. Too often, he would reach for his sleeve. Each time he sneezed, we would say, "God bless you." Then we'd encourage him to get a tissue or frantically try to get one to him before he wiped his nose on his shirt. Last week, Zachary had a cold and was sneezing often. There was a lot of blessing going on in our home. Sitting there one evening, he sneezed hard. He looked down at his arm and said, "Mommy, I've got God-bless-you all over my sleeve."

From *Mosaic Moments* by Lisa Copen

—◊◊◊—

I was saying a bedtime prayer with my seven-year-old granddaughter, Laura. The prayer was "Now I Lay Me Down to Sleep." After blessing Mommy, Daddy, two sisters, grandparents, aunts, uncles, cousins, friends, and pets, I said "Ahmen." Laura said, "Bless Aunt Minnie." I asked, "Who is Aunt Minnie?" Laura replied, "I don't know, but you said 'Aunt Min.'" I responded, "I said Ah-men." We both started laughing. Each night after that, we always blessed Aunt Minnie.

Mary Ellen Hornsby

—◊◊◊—

GOOD HOPES

BLESSINGS OF MANY FAITHS

Morning Song

As managers of a missionary guest house in Africa, we led blessings three times a day for eleven years. A good way to change things a bit was to sing our blessings, but since the composition of the group changed, not everyone always knew the words. Since this was a favorite, we solved the problem by making laminated place mats printed with these words. There they were, right in front of each of us. In the years following our stay in Africa, we've had many requests for this morning song.

I owe the Lord a morning song of gratitude and praise,
for the kind mercy He has shown in lengthening out my days.
He kept me safe another night; I see another day;
now may His Spirit, as the light, direct me in His way.
Keep me from danger and from sin; help me Thy will to do,
so that my heart be pure within; and I Thy goodness know.
Keep me till Thou wilt call me hence, where never night can be;
and save me, Lord, for Jesus' sake—He shed His blood for me.

Erma Lehman

Lord of one world,
bless us with the insight and foresight
to recognize our oneness,
to appreciate our interdependence,
to have the courage to explore our uniqueness,
to search for opportunities to see ourselves in one another,
to find joy in discovering a new unlikely friend,
to embrace the vision of peace,
to cherish our differences,
and most importantly,
to spread Your gift of love.

—⁓—

When you arise in the morning,
give thanks for the morning light,
for your life and strength.
Give thanks for your food
and the joy of living.
If you see no reason for giving thanks,
the fault lies in yourself.
Attributed to Tecumseh

—⁓—

Blessed are You, Lord our God, King of the universe,
who feeds the entire world in His goodness—
with grace, with kindness, and with mercy.
He gives food to all life, for His kindness is eternal.
Blessed are You, God, who nourishes all.
Jewish Blessing

—⁓—

May the Long Time Sun Shine Upon You
May the long time sun shine upon you.
All love surround you, and the pure light
within you guide you all the way on.
Yoga Chant

—⁓—

Come, Lord Jesus, our guest to be
and bless these gifts bestowed by Thee.
Be with our loved ones everywhere
and keep them ever in our care.
Moravian Blessing

—⁓—

O Great Spirit, whose voice I hear in the winds
and whose breath gives life to everyone, hear me.
I come to You as one of your many children;
I am weak . . . I am small . . . I need Your wisdom and Your strength.
Let me walk in beauty, and make my eyes ever behold
the red and purple sunsets.
Make my hands respect the things You have made,
and make my ears sharp so I may hear Your voice.
Make me wise, so that I may understand
what You have taught my people
and the lessons You have hidden in each leaf and each rock.
I ask for wisdom and strength,
not to be superior to my brothers,
but to be able to fight my greatest enemy, myself.
Make me ever ready to come before You
with clean hands and a straight eye,
so as life fades away as a fading sunset,
my spirit may come to You without shame.
Ojibwa Prayer

I ask nothing for myself,
but for others in the world
that are hungry or hurting in any way
that they will find peace, love, and wisdom.
May Lord Buddha guide you to all three.
Zen Prayer

—⟋⟍—

Hamotzi Lechem Min Ha'aretz
Baruch ata Adonai Elohenu Melech Ha'olam
Hamotzi Lechem Min Ha'aretz.
(Blessed are You O Lord our God,
Ruler of the universe,
who brings forth bread from the earth.)
Hebrew Blessing Over Bread

—⟋⟍—

A Blessing
Berachot 17a
Eruvin 54a

May your eyes sparkle with the light of Torah,
and may your ears hear the music of its words.
May the space between each letter of the scrolls
bring warmth and comfort to your soul.
May the syllables draw holiness from your heart,
and may this holiness be gentle and soothing
to you and all God's creatures.
May your study be passionate,
and meanings bear more meanings
until Life itself arrays itself to you
as a dazzling wedding feast.
And may your conversation,
even of the commonplace,
be a blessing to all who listen to your words
and see the Torah glowing on your face.
Danny Siegel
From *Unlocked Doors:*
The Selected Poetry of Danny Siegel, 1969–1983

—⁓—

A Native American Grace
O Morning Star!
When You look down upon us,
give us peace and refreshing sleep.
Great Spirit!
Bless our children, friends, and visitors
through a happy life.
May our trails lie straight and level before us.
Let us live to be old.
We are all Your children
and ask these things with good hearts.

—⁓—

(Sung to the tune of "Aloha Oy")
Aloha to God above
Aloha, a word that means
I love You.
Mahalo too means
I thank You.
Mahalo aloha to God.
Hawaiian Grace

—⁓—

Anglican Exhortation

Keep watch, dear Lord, with those who work, or watch, or weep this night,
and give Your angels charge over those who sleep. Tend the sick, Lord Christ;
give rest to the weary, bless the dying, soothe the suffering, pity the afflicted,
shield the joyous; and all for Your love's sake.

From *The Book of Common Prayer*

—~~—

The Buddhist Grace

This food is the gift of the whole universe—
the earth, the sky, and much hard work.
May we live in a way that is worthy of this food.
May we transform our unskillful states of mind, especially that of greed.
May we eat only foods that nourish us and prevent illness.
May we accept this food for the realization
of the way of understanding and love.

*In Buddhist monasteries before every meal, a monk or nun
recites these Five Contemplations.*

—~~—

Trail of Life Prayer

As I walk the trail of life in the fear of the wind and rain,
grant, O Great Spirit, that I may always walk like a man.

—⁓—

A Native American Thanksgiving

The Girl Scouts devised some wonderful
hand motions for this traditional blessing.
The eagle gives thanks for the mountains.
[Flap arms like wings, then become mountain peaks]
The fish give thanks for the sea.
[Hands together like swimming fish, then wave motion]
We give thanks for our blessings,
[Arms raised in front like receiving something
being passed down from a height]
And for what we're about to receive.
[Arms lowering, hands like they are holding something]

—⁓—

Nightcall

200

NANCY THOMP

BLESSINGS FOR FRIENDS AND FAMILY

When my identical twin sons passed their driving exams and received their long-awaited licenses, they had to accept with great disgust that Mom's law had requirements beyond the civil law. I insisted that each son drive five hundred miles with me before I would allow him to head out on his own.

When the day came for the boys' first solo flight on wheels, they walked through the kitchen door looking more like men than little boys. When I heard the engine turn over, I closed my eyes and searched my soul for peace, which came in the form of a blessing for those precious, naive young men. For the past six years, I have prayed it every day.

A Parent's Prayer for Teenage Drivers
Lord, go before and come behind.
Surround them with Your angels and
Keep them in Your care.
Jill M. Rigby

—∽∽—

A Prayer for Those We Love
I said a prayer for you today
and know God must have heard;
I felt the answer in my heart
although He spoke not a word.

I didn't ask for wealth or fame
(I knew you wouldn't mind);
I asked for priceless treasures rare
of a more lasting kind.

I prayed that He'd be near you
at the start of each new day,
to grant you health and blessings fair,
and friends to share your way.

I asked for happiness for you
in all things great and small,
but that you'd know His loving care
I prayed the most of all.
Frank Zamboni © 1979

—〰—

You're my friend, my companion,
through good times and bad.
My friend, my buddy,
through happy and sad.
Beside me you stand,
beside me you walk,
you're there to listen,
you're there to talk.
With happiness, with smiles,
with pain and tears,
I know you'll be there throughout the years!
You are all good friends to me,
and I am grateful to you.

—⁓—

I Wish for You
Comfort on difficult days,
smiles when sadness intrudes,
rainbows to follow the clouds,
laughter to kiss your lips,
sunsets to warm your heart,
gentle hugs when spirits sag,
friendships to brighten your being,
beauty for your eyes to see,
confidence for when you doubt,
faith so that you can believe,
courage to know yourself,
patience to accept the truth,
and love to complete your life.

—⁓—

A Mother's Prayer

O give me patience when little hands
tug at me with ceaseless small demands.
O give me gentle words and smiling eyes
and keep my lips from hasty sharp replies.
Let me not in weariness, confusion, or noise,
obscure my vision from life's few fleeting joys.
Then when in years to come, my home is still,
no bitter memories its rooms may fill.

—⁓⁓⁓—

God Bless You

I asked the Lord to bless you
as I prayed for you today;
to guide you and protect you
as you go along your way.
His love is always with you,
His promises are true;
you know in all your struggles
He will see you through.
So when the road you're traveling on
seems difficult at best,
take a moment, say a prayer,
and God will do the rest.

B. J. Morbitzer

—⁓⁓⁓—

Today

Today I wish you a day of ordinary miracles—
a fresh pot of coffee you didn't make yourself,
an unexpected phone call from an old friend,
green lights on your way to work.
I wish you a day of little things to rejoice in—
the fastest line at the grocery store,
a good song on the radio,
your keys right where you look.
I wish you a day of happiness and perfection—
little bite-sized pieces of perfection that give you
the funny feeling that the Lord is smiling on you,
holding you so gently because you are someone special and rare.
I wish you a day of peace, happiness, and joy!

—⁂—

Bless this house which is our home.
May we welcome all who come.

—⁂—

God bless all those that I love;
God bless all those that love me;
God bless all those that love those that I love
and all those that love those that love me!
From a New England sampler

—⁂—

I Wish You Enough

I wish you enough sun to keep your attitude bright.
I wish you enough rain to appreciate the sun more.
I wish you enough happiness to keep your spirit alive.
I wish you enough pain so that the smallest
joys in life appear much bigger.
I wish you enough gain to satisfy your wanting.
I wish you enough loss to appreciate all that you possess.
I wish you enough hellos to get through the final good-bye.
I wish you enough.

—⁓—

Blest Be the Tie that Binds

Blest be the tie that binds
our hearts in Christian love.
The fellowship of kindred minds
is like to that above.
Before our Father's throne
we pour our ardent prayers;
our fears, hope, our aims are one,
our comforts and our cares.
We share our mutual woes,
our mutual burdens bear,
and often for each other flows
the sympathizing tear.
John Fawcett

—⁓—

BLESSINGS FOR FRIENDS AND FAMILY

I pray for you that God give you
encouragement for overcoming obstacles,
wisdom to face challenging problems,
conviction for when you are uncertain,
and endurance to continue life's race.
May your heart be able to smile when sadness interferes.
May you see a rainbow in the cloudburst of the storm,
beauty of the sunset as the day darkens into night,
and joy in another's face offering a gift of friendship.
I pray that the Spirit of God gently hugs you when you are troubled
and warms your soul with a heavenly embrace
when you are chilled by the indifference of people.
And dear friend of mine, may you know the love of God
as you reach out to make easier a neighbor's burden,
to listen to a child's cry, to see the beauty of His nature,
and experience the splendor of His presence.
I pray that He blesses you,
and pours His glory into your life today.

—⁂—

Peace be to this house
and to all who dwell in it.
Peace be to them that enter
and to them that depart.

—⁂—

Miss . . . ! Miss . . . ! Miss . . . !
These days,
I am surrounded by little hands.
Little hands raising little fingertips
each vying,
stretching, trying
to reach my attention.

Each day,
it seems there is one more hand
than the last day,
one more hand,
with one more question,
one more search for knowledge ready to begin.

I see more hands
because I listen to more hands.
I talk with more hands
and I hold more hands
as I tell them that
each of their hands are special,
each of their hands are worth the time,
that each of their hands are needed
to make this world a better place.

So these days,
I walk around with my brain exposed
with everything I know exposed.
I dare each hand to grab
as much as their little hands can grab
so they will know and believe

that at least one person
knows and believes
that it is their smiles, their questions,
and their eager little hands
that have the power to
make this world a better place.
Melissa Mayes

—⚬⚬—

Prayer for Parents

Dear Heavenly Father, make me a better parent.
Teach me to understand my children,
to listen patiently to what they have to say
and to answer all their questions kindly.
Keep me from interrupting them,
talking back to them, and contradicting them.
Make me courteous to them, as I would have
them be to me. Give me the courage to confess my
sins against my children and to ask of them
forgiveness when I know that I have done them wrong.
May I not vainly hurt the feelings of my children.
Forbid that I should laugh at their mistakes
or resort to shame or ridicule as punishment.
Let me not tempt my child to lie and steal.
So guide me hour by hour that I may demonstrate
by all I say and do that honesty produces happiness.
Reduce, I pray the meanness in me.
May I cease to nag; and when I am out of sorts,
help me, O Lord, to hold my tongue.

—⚬⚬—

61

Prayer for Caretakers of Children with Attention-Deficit Hyperactivity Disorder

Lord, give them eyes to see into my child's heart
to recognize his goodness.
Give them ears to hear the laughter in her voice.
Let others see Your face when they look at my child.
Open their spirit and enable them to see past her
disorder and into her truly unique being.
Show them that You created this soul to fulfill
Your plans with unfailing love and guidance.
Bring all others into Your light
through these children's devotion to You, Lord.
Lord, lead these little sons and daughters to Your strength.
Teach them their own value and worth.
Show us, their parents and teachers, how to bring out their positive gifts.
Give us faith, hope, and joy through obstacles
overcome with Your all-powerful and merciful hand.
Alaine Benard

—ɯ—

Here's to good women:
May we know them.
May we raise them.
May we be them.

—ɯ—

Prayer for Loved One in Recovery
Dear Lord,
Please bless my loved one and give him this day of sobriety.
Increase his territory, Lord, for Your glory.
Be with him, Lord, put Your words in his
mouth that others may come to know You.
Keep Satan bound to the earth and away from my loved one.
Thank You, Jesus, for loving him so much. In Jesus' name I pray. Amen.

—⁓—

Prayer for a Daughter
Dear Lord,
May You always keep my little girl safe.
May You always keep her healthy.
May You always let her be good.
May You always let her be happy.
May You always keep her beautiful.
And may my prayers always be answered.
Jim Probsdorfer

—⁓—

BLESSINGS FOR HOLIDAYS AND SPECIAL OCCASIONS

I gave this wedding toast at a rehearsal dinner in Columbia, South Carolina, for the daughter of my childhood friend of more than fifty years. The toast was to convey the value and constancy of friendship, and its ability to survive years, distance, and travails, just like a strong marriage. The bond between my good friend and me is renewed annually by the exchange of a dime store birthday card—one we've passed between us for forty-two years. I am sure this treasured tradition will continue until our deaths.

A Wedding Toast
May your marriage endure
and forever be strong.
May your hearts always be filled
with love's nurturing song.
May the joys that grow from your bond
always be sweet.

continued . . .

May your life's journey together
be long and complete.
Always be thankful for your families,
whom the both of you cherish.
Grow together like them,
ensuring such families
from this earth will not perish.
Show to all that your love,
the love between a woman and a man,
demonstrates forever,
a loving marriage is God's perfect plan.
Rick Donaldson

—⁂—

Advent Prayer
First the seed
and then the grain;
thank You, God,
for sun and rain.
First the flour
and then the bread;
thank You, God,
that we are fed.
Thank You, God,
for all Your care;
help us all
to share and share.
Lillian Cox

—⁂—

Thanksgiving Day Prayer
We take so much for granted
of life and liberty,
and think that we deserve it,
that all was done "for me."
Think how they must have struggled,
new pilgrims in this land.
So many died from hardships
yet still they made a stand.
When all the work was finished,
new crops sowed in the ground,
they gathered with their neighbors,
asked blessings all around.
O God, help us be grateful
for gifts You've sent our way.
For these we want to thank You
on this Thanksgiving day.
Kris Ediger

—⟫⟨—

An Old English New Year's Blessing
God bless thy year!
Thy coming in, thy going out
thy rest, thy traveling about;
the rough, the smooth,
the bright, the dear,
God bless thy year.

—⟫⟨—

Birthday Blessing

We thank Thee, heavenly Father,
for all thy mercies during the years that are past,
and pray for Thy continued blessing
through the days to come.
As Thou hast been mindful of us,
so make us always mindful of Thee.
Our times are in Thy hands,
and Thou art our hope and strength.
Do Thou, we beseech thee,
abide with us, guide and keep us
until at last we come to thine everlasting kingdom;
through Jesus Christ our Lord.
From *Prayers for All Occasions*

—⋙—

The Jelly Bean Prayer

Red is for the blood He gave.
Green is for the grass He made.
Yellow is for the sun so bright.
Orange is for the edge of night.
Black is for the grace He gave.
Purple is for the hour of grace.
Pink is for the new tomorrow.
A bag full of jelly beans,
colorful and sweet, is a prayer,
a promise, a special treat.
Happy Easter!
Shirley Kozak

—⋙—

A Bride's Prayer

O Father, my heart is filled with happiness
so wonderful that I am almost afraid.
This is my wedding day, and I pray Thee
that the beautiful joy of this day may never grow dim.
Rather, may its memories become more sweet and tender
with each passing anniversary. Thou has sent to me one
who seems all worthy of my deepest regard.
Grant unto me the power to keep him ever true and loving
as now. May I prove indeed a helpmate, a sweetheart,
a friend, and a steadfast guiding star along the temptations
that beset the impulsive hearts of man. Give me the skill
to make home the best loved place of all. Help me to
make its glow shine farther than any glare that would
dim its radiance. Let me, I pray Thee, meet the little
misunderstandings and cares of my new life bravely.
Be with me as I start on my mission of womanhood,
and keep my path from failure. Walk with us, even to the
end of our journey. Father, bless my wedding day,
hallow my marriage night, sanctify my motherhood—
if Thou seest fit to grant me that privilege.
And when all my youthful charms are faded,
and physical fascination give way to the greater charm of
blessed companionship, may we walk hand in hand down
the highway, lighted by the sunshine that comes from living
righteously for time and all eternity.

—⁂—

Native American Wedding Blessing

Now you will feel no rain,
for each of you will be shelter to the other.
Now you will feel no cold,
for each of you will be warmth to the other.
Now there is no more loneliness,
for each of you will be a companion to the other.
Now you are two bodies,
but there is one new life before you.

—⫘—

Mother's Day Prayer

Today we give special thanks to our mother,
whether here on earth or departed,
who has loved us and guided us
from infancy to maturity.
From *Table Graces: Prayers of Thanks*

—⫘—

Father's Day Prayer

On this special day
we remember what is true all year long,
that our fathers, through love and pride,
have helped us to become
responsible and loving human beings.
We are the better because of our fathers' guiding examples.
From *Table Graces: Prayers of Thanks*

—⫘—

A Father's Day Toast
To Dad,
May the love and respect we express
toward you make up for the worry and care
we have visited upon you.

—⋙—

Thanksgiving Grace
This is a day for thanks.
A day in which we see or hear or feel
the wonders of the other moments of the year.
This is a day for time.
A day in which we think of pasts
that make our present rich
and future bountiful.
This is a day for joy.
A day in which we share a gift of laughter
warm and gentle as a smile.
Above all, this is a day for peace.
So let us touch each other
and know that we are one.
For these and other blessings,
we thank Thee, God.
Daniel Roselle

—⋙—

Thanksgiving Grace

Lord, we humbly ask Thy blessing
on the turkey and the dressing,
on the yams and the cranberry jelly,
and the pickles from the deli.

Bless the apple pie and tea,
bless each and every calorie.
Let us enjoy Thanksgiving dinner.
Tomorrow we can all get thinner.

For all Thy help along the way
we're thankful this Thanksgiving day.
We're thankful too, for all our dear ones,
for all the far away and near ones.

Although we may be far apart,
we're together in our hearts.
Keep us in Thy loving care.
This is our Thanksgiving prayer.
P.S. Anyone who wishes
may help with the dishes.
Father Flanagan's Boys' Home

—⁓—

St. Patrick's Day Blessing

May the Irish hills caress you.
May her lakes and rivers bless you.
May the luck of the Irish enfold you.
May the blessings of St. Patrick behold you.

Thanksgiving Blessings
Lord be with us on this day of
Thanksgiving. Help us make the most of
this life we are living. As we are about to partake
of this bountiful meal let us not forget the needy
and the hunger they feel. Help us to show
compassion in all that we do, and for all our many
blessings, we say thank You.
Helen Latham

—⁓—

Our Wish to You
In the coming year may you have:
enough happiness to keep you sweet,
enough trials to keep you strong,
enough sorrow to keep you human,
enough hope to keep you happy,
enough failure to keep you humble,
enough success to keep you eager,
enough friends to give you comfort,
enough wealth to meet your needs,
enough enthusiasm to look forward,
enough faith to banish depression,
enough determination to make each day
a better day than yesterday.
Charlene Bailey Hardcastle

—⁓—

A Kwanzaa Commitment
(December 26–January 1)
Strive for discipline, dedication, and achievement in
all you do. Dare struggle and sacrifice and gain the strength
that comes from this. Build where you are and dare leave a
legacy that will last as long as the sun shines and the water flows.
Practice daily Umoja, Kujichagulia, Ujima, Ujamaa, Nia, Kuumba,
and Imani. And by the wisdom of the ancestors always walk
with us. May the year's end meet us laughing and stronger.
May our children honor us by following our example in love
and struggle. And at the end of the next year, may we sit
again together, in larger numbers, with greater achievement
and closer to liberation and a higher level of human life.
HARAMBEE! HARAMBEE!
Harambee! Harambee!
Harambee! Harambee!
Harambee!
Maulana Karenga
Dr. Maulana Karenga is the founder of Kwanzaa, a Pan-African holiday
celebrated throughout the world African community. He is also professor and
chair of the Department of Black Studies at California State University in Long Beach.

—⧉—

Tiny Tim's Toast
Here's to all!
God bless us every one!
Charles Dickens
From *A Christmas Carol*

—⧉—

Advent Table Prayer

After a moment of silence, a candle of the Advent wreath may be lit.
Leader: Maranatha! Come quickly!
Response: Maranatha! Come quickly!
Leader: Blessed are You, Lord, God
of all creation, in the darkness
and in the light. Blessed are You
in this food and in our sharing.
Blessed are You as we wait in
joyful hope for the coming of
our Savior, Jesus Christ.
Response: For the kingdom, the power,
and the glory are Yours,
now and forever.
(An Advent song may be sung now or after the meal.)

—⁓—

Christmastime Table Prayer

After a moment of silence, a candle or the Christmas tree may be lit.
Leader: Noel! Christ is born to us!
Response: Noel! O come let us adore!
Leader: Lord Jesus, in the peace of this
season our spirits rejoice. With the
animals and the angels,with the shepherd
and the stars, with Mary and Joseph, we
sing God's praise. By Your coming may
the hungry be filled with good things
and may our table and home be blessed.
Glory to God in the highest!
Response: And peace to God's people on earth!

BLESSINGS ON NATURE

In late fall, we spent the evening picking grapes, tiny ears of beautifully colored Indian corn, and lots of interestingly shaped gourds. I was very excited about the sweet grapes and the individual beauty of each ear of corn. I could not contain my amazement at God's wonderful creation. That night as we said our prayers, my four-year-old son, Austin, said, "And Mom, tell Him about the grapes . . . "

Arvilla Leis

—⁂—

Giver of all good things, we thank Thee:
for health and vigor,
for the air that gives the breath of life,
the sun that warms us,
and the good food that makes us strong,
for happy homes and for friends we love,
for all that makes it good to live.
Make us thankful, and eager to repay,
by cheerfulness and kindliness,
and by a readiness to help others.
Freely we have received; let us freely give,
in the name of Him who gave His life for us,
Jesus Christ our Lord.
From *Prayers for All Occasions*

The Garden

For the garden of your daily living,
come to the garden alone, while the dew is still on the roses . . .

Plant three rows of peas:
1. Peas of mind
2. Peas of heart
3. Peas of soul

Plant four rows of squash:
1. Squash gossip
2. Squash indifference
3. Squash grumbling
4. Squash selfishness

Plant four rows of lettuce:
1. Lettuce be faithful
2. Lettuce be kind
3. Lettuce be patient
4. Lettuce really love one another

No garden is without turnips:
1. Turnip for meetings
2. Turnip for service
3. Turnip to help one another

To conclude our garden we must have thyme:
1. Thyme for each other
2. Thyme for family
3. Thyme for friends

Water freely with patience and cultivate with love.
There is much fruit in your garden because you reap what you sow.

Let Us Give Thanks
For the gift of life, the air we breathe,
and the water we drink,
let us give thanks.
For the flowers and the trees and other plants
that beautify and sustain our lives,
and for the animals that sustain us
and reveal other forms of life to us,
let us give thanks.
For the food we eat, the houses that
shelter us, the clothing that protects us, and
for the family and friends who love and nurture us,
let us give thanks.
For our health and vitality,
let us give thanks.
For the ability to work and play,
for music and other forms of art that enhance
our spirit, for stories that widen our understanding
and appreciation for life, and for humor that refreshes,
let us give thanks.
Finally, for those who came
before us, both family and those we never knew,
who worked and sacrificed and even gave their lives
to make our way of living possible, and for the
opportunities to help others
and to make differences in their lives,
let us give thanks.

—⁄⁄⁄—

Festivals
Harvest time is gold and red:
thank You for our daily bread.
Christmas time is red and green:
heaven now on earth is seen.
Easter time is green and white:
bring us all to heaven's light.
Lois Rock

—⟩⟩⟩—

May today there be peace within.
May you trust God that you are exactly where
you are meant to be. May you not forget the infinite
possibilities that are born of faith. May you use those gifts
that you have received, and pass on the love that has
been given to you. . . . May you be content knowing that
you are a child of God. . . . Let His presence settle into your bones,
and allow your soul the freedom to sing, dance, praise,
and love. It is there for each and every one of us.
Saint Therese of Lisieux
Saint Therese of Lisieux is known as the Saint of Little Ways.
She believed in doing the little things in life with great love.
She is also known as the patron saint of flower growers and florists.
Represented by roses, she is also called the Little Flower.

—⟩⟩⟩—

Father, We Thank Thee
For flowers that bloom about our feet,
Father, we thank Thee.
For tender grass so fresh, so sweet,
Father, we thank Thee.
For the song of bird and hum of bee,
for all things fair we hear or see,
Father in heaven, we thank Thee.
For blue of stream and blue of sky,
Father, we thank Thee.
For pleasant shade of branches high,
Father, we thank Thee.
For fragrant air and cooling breeze,
for the beauty of the blooming trees,
Father in heaven, we thank Thee.
For this new morning with its light,
Father, we thank Thee.
For rest and shelter of the night,
Father, we thank Thee.
For health and food, for love and friends,
For everything Thy goodness sends,
Father in heaven, we thank Thee.

—⁂—

Thank God, who sends the gentle rain
that thirsty flowers may drink again,
for puddles on the garden path,
where little birds may take a bath.
A. W. I. Chitty

Thank You, God, for autumn days,
with shining fields and golden sheaves
and ripening fruits and rustling leaves,
for corn and flour and new-made bread,
and golden butter quickly spread.
Thank You for the friendly cow
who gives us milk to make us grow;
for woolly sheep and clothing warm
to keep us all from cold and harm;
for nuts and fruits and berries red,
upon the trees and bushes spread.
Man and child and beast and bird
say, "Thank You very much, dear God."
Mary Osborn

—⁄⁄⁄—

For the golden corn,
for the apples on the tree,
for the golden butter
and the honey for our tea;
for fruits and nuts and berries
that grow beside the way,
for birds and beasts and flowers
we thank Thee ev'ry day.

—⁄⁄⁄—

Green Things
Dear God in paradise
look upon our sowing;
bless the little gardens
and the green things growing.

—⟋⟍—

God Made the Sun
God made the sun
and God made the tree;
God made the mountains,
and God made me.

—⟋⟍—

The Changing Seasons
Praise the Lord for all the seasons.
Praise Him for the gentle spring.
Praise the Lord for glorious summer,
birds and beasts and everything.
Praise the Lord, who sends the harvest.
Praise Him for the winter snows.
Praise the Lord, all ye who love Him.
Praise Him, for all things He knows.

—⟋⟍—

Pumpkin Seeds

Sometimes I think that my life is a lot like a pumpkin seed. Many years ago I took a pumpkin seed, one of God's ugliest seeds, and planted it in the earth. In a few days it sprouted two green leaves. I chopped, tilled, watered, and fed it. The rain fell on it, and I tilled it again, and soon I had a long vine with blooms on it growing everywhere. By Halloween time I had two pumpkins, one small and one large.

I made a snaggle-toothed jack 'o lantern out of the big one, scooping it out through the cut-off top and placing a broken candle inside. When I called the children in to see it, they could see the light of life shining in its ugly face. I peeled and cooked the other pumpkin and made pies and bread, which I shared with neighbors and some of the sick and shut-ins.

But I still had all of these seeds left, so I put them in a pan out on the back steps. As I looked out the window later, I saw a bird, a squirrel, a butterfly, and even a bumblebee come and sit on the seeds. And I said to myself, "Heavenly Father, look what Your ugly seeds have done. They have made children, my neighbors, the sick, the birds, bees, squirrels, and butterflies all happy."

This made me realize something I have thought about so many times since. My life, through this pumpkin seed, brought so much happiness and joy. Like the pumpkin seed, my life can continue to bring happiness and joy to others. When I plant my garden in the spring, I do it with the thought that one single bean can create so many new beans—half a pound or more. How many plants will come from one bean if you chop it, feed it, and water it?

Mildred Council
From *Mama Dip's Kitchen*

—ᗰ—

Heavenly God,
help us to see the beautiful things in earth and sky,
which are tokens of Your love. Walk with us in the days we
spend together here. May the food we eat and all Your
blessings help us to better serve You and each other.
From the *Boy Scout Camp Chickahominy Interfaith Worship Service*

—〰—

Thank You
Thank You for all my hands can hold—
apples red and melons gold,
yellow corn both ripe and sweet,
peas and beans so good to eat!
Thank You for all my eyes can see—
lovely sunlight, field, and tree,
white cloud-boats in sea-deep sky,
soaring bird and butterfly.
Thank You for all my ears can hear—
birds' songs echoing far and near,
songs of little stream, big sea,
cricket, bullfrog, duck, and bee.
Ivy O. Eastwick

—〰—

For dawn of gray and tattered sky,
for silver rain on grass and tree;
for song and laughter
and work well done,
our thankful hearts we raise to Thee.

BLESSINGS FOR AMERICA AND OUR MILITARY

Julie Huggins and Lee Hayden are friends who are military wives. Julie has been a military wife for twenty-five years. She has supported her husband in his service to our country and has been an active community volunteer at each stop in his career. The author of this poem is unknown, but Julie found it particularly meaningful and shared it with Lee.

Thank You, Lord, for This Soldier That I Love
Thank You, Lord, for this soldier that I love.
Give me Your strength and compassion
to endure the trials and challenges of military life.
Let Your unconditional love fill me
that I may be a soul mate, a lover, and a friend.
Be a shield to keep him/her
safe during the everyday battles of life.
Direct his/her steps, Lord, that through
him/her Your grace may be seen.
Thank You for our marriage—
may it be a source of joy in Your eyes.

continued . . .

Lee says, "As you can imagine, many military wives keep copies of this prayer close at hand. Our husbands, salesmen and defenders of freedom, are a special breed. Our fellow countrymen must remember to be thankful for those who have served in the past, those who presently serve, and for the young men and women who will serve in the future."

She continues, "My husband, Col. David Hayden, was deployed to Afghanistan, May 2002–April 2003. It was a very difficult time in our country, the world, and especially the army post where we lived, Fort Bragg, North Carolina, as many families had loved ones in dangerous and distant lands. We were fortunate to have e-mail access and could communicate with one another. This prayer, sent to me by another army spouse, was by my computer and I repeated it each night as I sat to write to him."

Army Wife's Prayer
Dear Lord, give me greatness of heart to see
the difference between duty and his love for me.
Give me understanding that I may know,
when duty calls him, he must go.
Give me a task to do each day
to fill the time when he's away.
Lord, when he's in a foreign land,
keep him safe in Your loving hand.
Lord, when duty is in the field,
please protect him and be his shield.
And Lord, when deployment is so long,
please stay with me and keep me strong.
Amen.
Julie Huggins and Lee Hayden

—〰—

Heavenly Father, in the beginning You created us to be free, to exercise the right of choice with all the responsibilities such privilege requires. We indeed are thankful for every blessing You have given us. Today, we are especially grateful for Your love expressed through the freedom we enjoy as individuals and as a nation. Remember, Lord, those who sacrificed to make our independence a reality. Bless us as we strive to preserve the heritage they left us. May our efforts lead to peace among the nations of the world.

From the United States Air Force Chaplain *Book of Prayers*

—⟋⟍—

Abraham Lincoln's 1863 Blessing

It is the duty of nations, as well as of men, to owe their dependence upon the overruling power of God, to confess their sins and transgressions in humble sorrow, yet with assured hope that genuine repentance will lead to mercy and pardon; and to recognize the sublime truth, announced in the Holy Scriptures and proven by all history, that those nations only are blessed whose God is the Lord.

This blessing from President Lincoln appears to be based on Psalm 33:12
and 2 Chronicles 7:14. It calls on God's promise to bless a nation
that will humble itself in repentance over its corporate sin.

—⟋⟍—

Psalm 107:23–30

May God bless this ship and all who sail in her. Amen.

—⟋⟍—

America the Beautiful
O beautiful for spacious skies,
for amber waves of grain,
for purple mountain majesties
above the fruited plains.
America! America!
God shed His grace on thee,
and crown thy good with brotherhood
from sea to shinning sea.

O beautiful for pilgrim feet
whose stern impassioned stress
a thoroughfare for freedom breath
across the wilderness!
America! America!
God mend thy every flaw.
Confirm thy soul in self-control,
thy liberty in law.

O beautiful for heroes proved
in liberating strife
who more than self their country loved,
and mercy more than life!
America! America!
May God thy gold refine.
Till all success is nobleness
and every gain divine!

O beautiful for patriot dream
that sees beyond the years
thine alabaster cities gleam
undimmed by human tears!
America! America!
God shed His grace on thee,
and crown thy good with brotherhood
from sea to shinning sea.
C. L. Bates and S. A. Ward

—⌇⌇—

Lord, hold our troops in Your loving hands.
Protect them as they protect us.
Bless them and their families for the selfless acts
they perform for us in our time of need.
In the name of Jesus, Our Lord and Savior.

—⌇⌇—

O Lord, we pray for America, thanking You for our forefathers whom You mercifully guided in building this beautiful nation—a nation indivisible, with liberty and justice for all. We pray humbly for all those men and women who, with faith in You and their country, gave themselves for our freedom. In memory of them, give us a passionate determination to be instruments of peace among the nations of the world. Let our hope today be America the beautiful, one nation under God.
From the United States Air Force Chaplain *Book of Prayers*

—⌇⌇—

Grant us peace, Thy most precious gift,
O thou eternal source of peace,
and enable Israel to be its messenger
unto the peoples of the earth.
Bless our country
that it may ever be a stronghold of peace,
and its advocate in the council of nations.
May contentment reign within its borders,
health and happiness within its homes.
Strengthen the bonds of friendship and fellowship
among the inhabitants of all lands.
Plant virtue in every soul,
and may the love of Thy name
hallow every home and every heart.
Praised be Thou, O Lord, giver of peace.
From *Union Prayer Book*

———

Our heavenly Father, we bow before You as the one perfect source of all wisdom, goodness, and mercy. Teach us to be wise in ways that exalt truth, fidelity, and honor. Instill within us a passion for human service and an ambition to contribute to the greater good of our nation. May right and justice ever be cornerstones of our free society. Bless our country and continue to strengthen us with the ideals of her founders.
From the United States Air Force Chaplain *Book of Prayers*

———

Prayer for America
Gracious God, all that we have and are
is a result of your amazing generosity.
Since September 11, in the battle against terrorism,
we have discovered again that You truly are
our refuge and strength, an ever-present help in trouble.
We rededicate ourselves to be one nation under You.
In You we trust.
We reaffirm our accountability to you,
to the absolutes of Your commandments
and to justice in our society.
Bless our president, Congress, and all our leaders
with Your supernatural power.
We commit ourselves to be faithful to You
as Sovereign of our land and as our personal Lord and Savior.
Dr. Lloyd Ogilvie, former Chaplain of the United States Senate

—⁓—

Father, we commend our nation to Your merciful care, that being guided by Your providence, we may dwell secure in Your peace. Grant to the president of the United States, members of his administration, Congress, and all in authority wisdom and strength to know and do Your will. Help them by the power of Your Holy Spirit to formulate laws and policies that advance the cause of justice and peace. May our leaders be ever mindful of their calling to serve instead of being served. May Your commandments be their guide. And grant that both rulers and people will serve You with one mind and heart.
From the United States Air Force Chaplain *Book of Prayers*

—⁓—

It Is the Veteran

It is the veteran, not the preacher,
who has given us freedom of religion.

It is the veteran, not the reporter,
who has given us freedom of the press.

It is the veteran, not the poet,
who has given us freedom of speech.

It is the veteran, not the campus organizer,
who has given us freedom to assemble.

It is the veteran, not the lawyer,
who has given us the right to a fair trial.

It is the veteran, not the politician,
Who has given us the right to vote.

It is the veteran, who salutes the flag,
who serves under the flag.

Eternal rest grant them, O Lord,
and let light perpetual shine upon them.

—⁄⁄⁄—

Celtic/Gaelic Ship's Blessing

Helmsman (H): Bless our ship.

Sailors (S): May God the Father bless her.

H: Bless our ship.

S: May Jesus Christ bless her.

H: Bless our ship.

S: May the Holy Ghost bless her.

H: What fear ye when God the Father is with you?

S: We fear no evil.

H: What fear ye when God the Son is with you?

S: We fear no evil.

H: What fear ye when God the Holy Ghost is with you?

S: We fear no evil.

Helmsman:

May God, Almighty Father, with the love of His Son Christ Jesus and the comfort of the Holy Ghost, One God, who miraculously led the children of Israel through the Red Sea, who took Jonah to dry land in the belly of the great whale, who delivered the apostle Paul and his helpless ship from the raging and boisterous sea, save us and defend us and bless us and guide us prosperously and cheerfully and with joy on the wide sea and lead us to our quiet haven according to His own divine will.

This old Celtic/Gaelic ship's blessing came from the island of Iona in the Hebrides. It was printed in 1837 and was entitled The Blessing of the Ship *by John McCormick and William Muir. In their preface, the authors explain that the blessing had been said for centuries by sailors as they set sail on a voyage. They took their version from the sixteenth-century liturgy composed by John Kersewell, Bishop of Argyll.*

—⁂—

Ship's Blessing

They that go down to the sea in ships,
that do business in great waters;

These see the works of the LORD,
and His wonders in the deep.

For He commandth, and raiseth the stormy wind,
which lifteth up the waves thereof.

They mount up to the heaven,
they go down again to the depths.
Their soul is melted because of trouble.

They reel to and fro
and stagger like a drunken man,
and are at their wits' end.

Then they cry unto the LORD in their trouble,
and He bringeth them out of their distresses.

He maketh the storm a calm,
so that the waves thereof are still.

Then are they glad because they be quiet;
so He bringeth them unto their desired haven.

This blessing was submitted by the Jamestown-Yorktown Foundation staff.
It was the blessing said over the new replica of the seventeenth-century
sailing ship, The Godspeed. *The* Godspeed *represents one of three ships*
that landed at Jamestown in 1607, bringing settlers to America.

—⚓—

In 2004, my son telephoned me from Iraq. We were discussing his hectic life when he announced he had to say good-bye because they were being bombed. I ran downstairs praying and turned on the television to one of those news channels. I saw what looked like a sandy floor in a very plain chapel. Along the bottom of the screen in white letters were the words "The Lord seeketh." At that moment, I experienced a total peace and knew my son was all right. Ten minutes later, he called and stated, "I'm fine. Got to go."

Christina N. Helwig

—⁄⁄⁄—

Our Father, as we turn our thoughts to Thee,
Cleanse our hearts from strain and strife
that we may one day worthy be
To break with Thee the bread of life.
Blessing attributed to Confederate General George Edward Pickett

—⁄⁄⁄—

Lord, we thank You for America and for the virtues of democracy—virtues which ensure liberty and justice throughout the land. Our nation is one blessed with freedom and hope. Guide us in our efforts to live in peace. Spare us from attitudes which detract from our heritage. Affirm in us our dependence upon You and instill within us courage to serve You faithfully. Bless those who lead us with wisdom. May our efforts to defend liberty illumine the way of peace and bring happiness to all.

From the United States Air Force Chaplain *Book of Prayers*

—⁄⁄⁄—

BLESSINGS FOR ANIMALS

Patty was my first kitten—I even got to see her squirm her way into the world. Tiny, gray, and with a black-outlined pink nose, she and I soon became inseparable. She slept at my side, my feet, or so close to my head, she might have been a hat. She came when I called, nudging my nose with hers, flopping down into my lap, and purring so loudly that she produced an echo through the house. She was always there. She was my best friend for fourteen years, and although that seems so short, memories of her are forever in my heart. Remembering her, I realize what a blessing God gives us when He sends those loyal, furry, perfect little companions. When God gave me Patty, He gave me someone who loved me and who would be my friend when I felt I had no one else. "The Rainbow Bridge" reminds me that Patty and I will meet again. As I remember her and look at my current animal companions, I can't help but thank God for giving us a piece of His love that we can physically hold.

LeAnna Massingille

Rainbow Bridge

Just this side of heaven is a place called Rainbow Bridge.
When an animal dies that has been especially close to someone here,
that pet goes to Rainbow Bridge.
There are meadows and hills for all of our special friends

99

continued . . .

so they can run and play together.
There is plenty of food, water, and sunshine,
and our friends are warm and comfortable.
All the animals who had been ill and old
are restored to health and vigor;
those who were hurt or maimed are made
whole and strong again, just as we remember them
in our dreams of days and times gone by.
The animals are happy and content, except for one small thing;
they each miss someone very special to them, who had to be left behind.
They all run and play together, but the day comes when one
suddenly stops and looks into the distance.
His bright eyes are intent; his eager body quivers.
Suddenly he begins to run from the group, flying over the
green grass, his legs carrying him faster and faster.
You have been spotted, and when you and your special friend finally meet,
you cling together in joyous reunion, never to be parted again.
The happy kisses rain upon your face; your hands again caress the beloved head,
and you look once more into the trusting eyes of your pet,
so long gone from your life but never absent from your heart.
Then you cross Rainbow Bridge together. . . .

—⁓—

O heavenly Father,
protect and bless all things that have breath;
guard them from all evil, and let them sleep in peace.
Albert Schweitzer

—⁓—

Death Is Nothing at All

Death is nothing at all.
I have only slipped into the next room.
I am I and you are you.
And the old life that we lived,
Whatever we were to each other,
that we are still.
Call me by my old familiar name.
Speak to me in the easy way you always used.
Put no difference into your tone.
Wear no forced air of solemnity or sorrow.
Laugh as we always laughed
at the little jokes
we always enjoyed together.
Play, smile, think of me, pray for me.
Let my name be ever the household name that it always was.
Let it be spoken without effort,
Without the ghost of a shadow in it.
Life means all that it ever meant.
It is the same as it ever was.
There is an absolute unbroken continuity.
What is death but a negligible accident?
Why should I be out of mind
Because I am out of sight?
I am waiting for you for an interval,
somewhere very near,
just around the corner.
All is well.

Canon Henry Scott-Holland

Many animal lovers find solace in this elegant blessing originally written as part of a sermon by Canon Henry Scott-Holland of St. Paul's Cathedral in London.

Member of the Family

What would I do without you,
My precious, furry friend? . . .
Part mischief, but all blessing,
And faithful to the end!

You look at me with eyes of love;
You never hold a grudge . . .
You think I'm far too wonderful
To criticize or judge.

It seems your greatest joy in life
Is being close to me . . .
I think God knew how comforting
Your warm, soft fur would be.

I know you think you're human,
But I'm glad it isn't true . . .
The world would be a nicer place
If folks were more like you!

A few short years are all we have;
One day we'll have to part . . .
But you, my pet, will always have
A place within my heart.

Hope Harrington Kolb, © 1993

—ᴧᴧᴧ—

Blessing for Pets

Blessed are You, Lord God, maker of all living creatures.
You called forth fish in the sea, birds in the air, and animals on the land.
You inspired St. Francis to call all of them his brothers and sisters.
We ask You to bless this pet.
By the power of Your love, enable it to live according to your plan.
May we always praise You for all Your beauty in creation.
Blessed are You, Lord our God, in all Your creatures! Amen.

Franciscan Prayer

—⁂—

The Twenty-Third Psalm for Cat Owners

I am your servant.
You shall not want me.
You maketh me to lie down where cat hair abounds,
you leadeth me to pricey pet stores for toys and trinkets
to amuse and adorn your inner kitten.
You guideth me to sunny spots for afternoon naps.
Yea, even though you walk on the kitchen counters,
fear neither rod nor staff, for thou art my heart's meow.
I prepareth a feast before you
to tempt your capricious appetite.
I brush your coat with gentle strokes.
I dispose of your repugnant hairballs with practiced aplomb.
My indulgence overfloweth.
Surely warmth and purring shall follow you
all the days of your nine lives
and we will dwell in mutual affection
in the house that once was mine.

Susan J. Erickson

HUMOROUS BLESSINGS

Our four boys and two girls detested English peas, which their father and I enjoyed eating. I was always trying to disguise them in hopes that the children would learn to eat and enjoy them as well. Needless to say, I was never successful.

In our family, each child took turns saying a blessing at dinner. One evening, when it was Jeff's turn to pray, off the tip of his four- or five-year-old tongue came this blessing:

> Dear Lord,
> Please bless all of this food
> except those little green peas
> at the end of the table.
> Could You maybe
> make them taste like jelly beans? Amen.

I finally gave up and stopped trying to tempt them into eating little green peas, which I surely could never transform into tasting like jelly beans.

Rae Spigener

—✴—

The Twenty-Third Psalm for the Workplace
The Lord is my real boss,
and I shall not want.
He gives me peace
when chaos is all around me.
He gently reminds me to pray
before I speak and
to do all things without murmuring
and complaining.
He reminds me that He is my
source and not my job.
He restores my sanity every day and
guides my decisions
that I might honor Him
in everything I do.
Even though I face absurd amounts
of e-mail, system crashes,
unrealistic deadlines, budget cutbacks,
gossiping coworkers, discriminating supervisors,
and an aging body that doesn't
cooperate every morning,
I will not stop—for He is with me!
His presence, His peace,
and His power will see me through.
He raises me up, even when they
fail to promote me.
He claims me as His own,
even when the company
threatens to let me go.
His faithfulness and love are better than

any bonus check,
and His retirement plan
beats every 401K there is!
When it's all said and done,
I'll be working for Him a whole lot longer,
and for that, I bless His name.

—⁓—

So far today, God,
I've done all right.
I haven't gossiped.
I haven't lost my temper,
been grumpy, nasty, or selfish.
I am really glad of that.
But in a few moments, God,
I'm going to get out of bed,
and from then on I'm going
to need a lot of your help.

—⁓—

I eat my peas with honey,
I have done so all my life.
It makes the peas taste funny,
but it keeps them on my knife.
Thank you, heavenly Father.
*Following the blessing at every family holiday meal, my
great-uncle Reed Polland would say the above verse.*
Shelly Richardson Scott

—⁓—

A man was asked if you must kneel to say a prayer.
"No," he said. "The best prayer I ever prayed,
I was stuck head downward in a well."

—⟋⟋⟍—

Lord, my soul is sipped with riot,
incited by a wicked diet!
"You are what you eat!" said a wise old man,
and Lord, if it's true, then I'm a garbage can.
Give me this day my daily slice,
but cut it thin and toast it twice.
I pray each night with heavy prayers,
deliver me from chocolate eclairs.
And when my days of trial are done,
and my war with malted milk is won,
let me stand so proud with the saints in heaven,
in a shiny robe, size six or seven.
I can do it, Lord, if You'll show to me,
the virtues of lettuce and celery.
If You'll teach the evil of mayonnaise,
the sinfulness of hollandaise,
and crisp fried chicken from down South,
Lord, if You love me—*shut my mouth!*

—⟋⟋⟍—

Dear Lord,
If You can't make me thin,
make my friends—fat!
Amen.

Now I lay me
down to sleep.
I pray the Lord
my shape to keep.
Please no wrinkles,
please no bags,
and please lift my butt
before it sags.
Please no age spots,
please no gray.
And as for my belly,
please take it away.
Please keep me young,
and thank You, dear Lord,
for all that You've done.

—◆—

Holy, Holy, Holy Lord God of hosts.
Blessed is He who comes in the name of the Lord.
Lasagna (Hosanna) in the highest.
**Recited by a first grader to
Sister David Ann Niski, Bernardine Foundation**

—◆—

Dusting

Dust if you must but wouldn't it be better,
to paint a picture or write a letter,
bake a cake or plant a seed,
ponder the difference between want and need?
Dust if you must but there's not much time,
with rivers to swim and mountains to climb,
music to hear and books to read,
friends to cherish and life to lead.
Dust if you must but the world's out there,
with the sun in your eyes, the wind in your hair,
a flutter of snow, a shower of rain.
This day will not come around again.
Dust if you must but bear in mind,
old age will come and it's not kind.
And when you go and go you must,
you, yourself, will make more dust.

—⁂—

God bless all men and some women.
*Prayed by a young girl who evidently
misheard "amen" as "all men".*

—⁂—

The Twenty-Third Psalm for Busy People
The Lord is my pacesetter; I shall not rush;
He makes me stop and rest for quiet intervals,
He provides me with images of stillness
which restore my serenity.
He leads me in the way of efficiency,
through calmness of mind;
and His guidance is peace.
Even though I have a great many things to accomplish each day,
I will not fret, for His presence is here.
His timelessness, His all-importance will keep me in balance.
He prepares refreshment and renewal in the midst of activity,
by anointing my mind with His oils of tranquility.
My cup of joyous energy overflows.
Surely harmony and effectiveness shall
be the fruits of my hours.
And I shall walk in the pace of my Lord,
and dwell in His house forever.
Toki Miyashina

*Psalm Twenty-three, "The Lord is my Shepherd," has probably been set to music
and paraphrased more than any other part of the Bible. This modern version from Japan
gives it a new impact for today's readers—especially those who live in the city.*

111

SOURCES

Where noted, blessings are printed with permission from the following sources:

Beilenson, Nick, ed. *Table Graces: Prayers of Thanks*. White Plains, N.Y.: Peter Pauper Press, 1986.

Copen, Lisa J. *Mosaic Moments: Devotionals for the Chronically Ill*. San Diego, Calif.: Rest Ministries, Inc., 2003.

Council, Mildred. *Mama Dip's Kitchen*. Chapel Hill, N.C.: University of North Carolina Press, 1999.

Department of the Air Force Chaplain Service. *Book of Prayers*. Air University Gunter Air Force Base, Ala.: United States Chaplain Service Resource Board, 1991.

Gates of Prayer: The New Union Prayerbook. New York: Central Conference of American Rabbis, 1975.

Lentz, Gail S. *Hope for the Healing Heart*. Self Published, 1998.

McCormick, John and William Muir. *The Blessing of the Ship*. Iona, J. McCormick and W. Muir, 1887.

Prayers for All Occasions. Cincinnati, Ohio: Forward Movement Publications, 1964.

Siegel, Danny. *Unlocked Doors: The Selected Poems of Danny Siegel*, 1969–1983. Pittsboro, N.C.: The Town House Press,1983.

Tripp, Diane Karay. *Prayers from the Reformed Tradition*. Louisville, Ky.: Witherspoon Press, 2001.

ABOUT THE JUNIOR LEAGUE OF HAMPTON ROADS, INC.

The Junior League of Hampton Roads, Inc. is an organization of women committed to promoting voluntarism, developing the potential of women, and improving the community through the effective action and leadership of trained volunteers. Its purpose is exclusively educational and charitable.

The Junior League of Hampton Roads, founded in 1949, is an organization of more than four hundred women who all share a common goal of community improvement. The Junior League reaches out to all women from the communities of Gloucester, Hampton, Newport News, Poquoson, Williamsburg, Smithfield, and Isle of Wight to join as members. The League is affiliated with 293 Leagues internationally, representing 170,000 women.

The Junior League of Hampton Roads's projects would never come to fruition without the generous support of its own members and like-minded community volunteers. Since its beginning, hundreds of thousands of dollars have been contributed to various community efforts such as Peninsula Youth Home, Kids on the Block, The Grants Resource Library, Peninsula Fine Arts Center, The Volunteer Center, and The Virginia Living Museum. All proceeds from the sales of this book will be returned to the community through the many League projects and services.

AUTHORS AND CONTRIBUTORS

Rosemary & Jeff Adams
Nancy A. Allen
Nancy J. Allen
E. J. Allen-Williams
Mary Anderson
Sally Sue Andrews
Sue Anna Barrett
C. L. Bates
Anthony Bell
Faith Belote
Alaine Benard
Senator Daniel W. "Danny" Bird Jr.
Sister Marie Blanchette
The Bowditch Family
    of Yorktown
Marian Hornsby Bowditch
Chaplain Marie Boyd
Judi Braddy
Gail Branum
Amy Broad
Eleanor Weston Brown
The Reverend
    Douglas G. Burgoyne
Kim Campbell
Tom Carmine
Lyles Carr
John Cennick
The Children of Father
    Flanagan's Boys' Home
The Reverend George Chioros
A. W. I. Chitty
Robert W. Clayton
Colonial Virginia Council of the
    Boy Scouts of America

Commonwealth Nursing
    & Hospice
Dr. Audrey Cook
Minette Cooper
DeeDee Copeland
Lisa Copen
Mildred Council
Lillian Cox
Lea Crissman
Susan Danish
Carolyn Dawkins
Charles Dickens
Sandy & Rick Donaldson
Letia Drewry
Mary Lou Duberg
Lynn Dunagan
Rabbi Scott Durdin
Elsie DuVal
Ivy O. Eastwick
Kris Ediger
Phil Emerson
Adam Emory
Ann M. Engle
Susan J. Erickson
Patricia Evans
John Fawcett
Karen Fetzer
Rachel Field
A. S. T. Fisher
Margaret Fluharty
Saint Francis of Assisi
Tyra & Dr. John Freed
Captain Peter N. Fischer
Maryleona Frost

Peter Gaines
Mackenzie Gardner
Maxine Garvalia
Linda Gilden
Barbara Glanz, CSP
Judy Goad
Rabbi Norman Golner
Josh Grami
Carolyn Griffin
Charlene Bailey Hardcastle
Andrea Harley
Lee Hayden
Christina N. Helwig
Missy Hespenhide
Craig Hill, Family Foundations
    International
Dr. Carolyn Hines
Mary Ellen Hornsby
Kimberly Howell
The Hudgins Family
Anne Huffman
Margaret Anne Huffman
Julie Huggins
Doris H. Hunt
Molly Hunter
The Iona Community
Kathryn Jacobs
Jamestown-Yorktown
    Foundation
Nancy J. Jenkins
Emilie Fendall Johnson
Mary Jo Johnson
Allen J. Jones
Michele Woods Jones

Sidney Jordan
Junior League of Baltimore, Inc.
Jill Keech
Maulana Kerenga
Hope Harrington Kolb
Shirley Kozak
Caroline, Hunter, & Molly Lash
Helen Latham
Mary A. Lathbury
Edith Rutter Leatham
Judy Lee
Erma Lehman
Arvilla, Austin, & Jim Leis
Gail S. Lentz
Abraham Lincoln
Susan Lineberry
Hayven Livers
Joan Loock
Martin Luther
Gavin & Alison MacCleery
Michael Mappin
Dorothy Marshall
The Reverend
   Dr. Robert D. Marston
LeAnna Massingille
Melissa Mayes
Carol McCabe
John McCormick
Emily Miles
Betsy Miller
Anne Millner
Toki Miyashina
B. J. Morbitzer
Thomas Moore

William Muir
W. H. Neidlinger
Sister David Ann Niski
Josie O'Connor
Dr. Lloyd Ogilvie
Mary Osborn
Mary Lou Osborn
Donna Owens
Margaret Patterson
Robertson Peters
Celestine Phillips
General George Edward Pickett
Arlissa Powell
Laurine Press
Jim Probsdorfer
John V. Quarstein
Lola Raney
Mary Jo Raney
The Reverend Melanie C. Reuter
Jill M. Rigby
Robin Roberts
Mrs. L. C. "Ruby" Robertson Sr.
Shari-Ann Robertson
Lois Rock
Daniel Roselle
Trish Rucker-Dempsey
The Reverend
   Howard W. Saunders III
Albert Schweitzer
Shelby Richardson Scott
Canon Henry Scott-Holland
The Seaton Family
Ed Sharpe
Danny Siegel

Rae Spigener
Kimberly Stubbs
Lee Summerell
Dr. Calvin H. Sydnor III
Tecumseh
Mother Teresa
David Joseph Tetrault
Saint Therese of Lisieux
Shane Thomas
Rosemary Trible
Karen Westerfield Tucker
U.S. Air Force Chaplain Service
Henry J. van Dyke
June Varnum
Joan Verrhoef
Virginia Foundation of
   Independent Colleges
Herb Wagner
Eda Lous Walton
S. A. Ward
Liz Waters
Judy & Bob Weikle
Chase Whitney
Suzannah (Susie) Wornom
Frank Zamboni

ABOUT THE ARTIST

Nancy Thomas is a nationally known contemporary artist who has lived and painted in historic Yorktown, Virginia, for more than thirty years. Her work is prized throughout the country for its wonderful color, warmth, and style. Nancy's art appears in the homes of thousands of collectors. It also appears in magazines, decorator books, museums, and Hollywood films, and on Broadway and on television.

Nancy has given one-woman shows across America and abroad, and has been commissioned for numerous special works by a variety of institutions, including Colonial Williamsburg, the Museum of American Folk Art, and the White House.

The Junior League of Hampton Roads, Inc. is honored that Nancy Thomas graciously donated her creativity and art to *Blessings We Celebrate*.

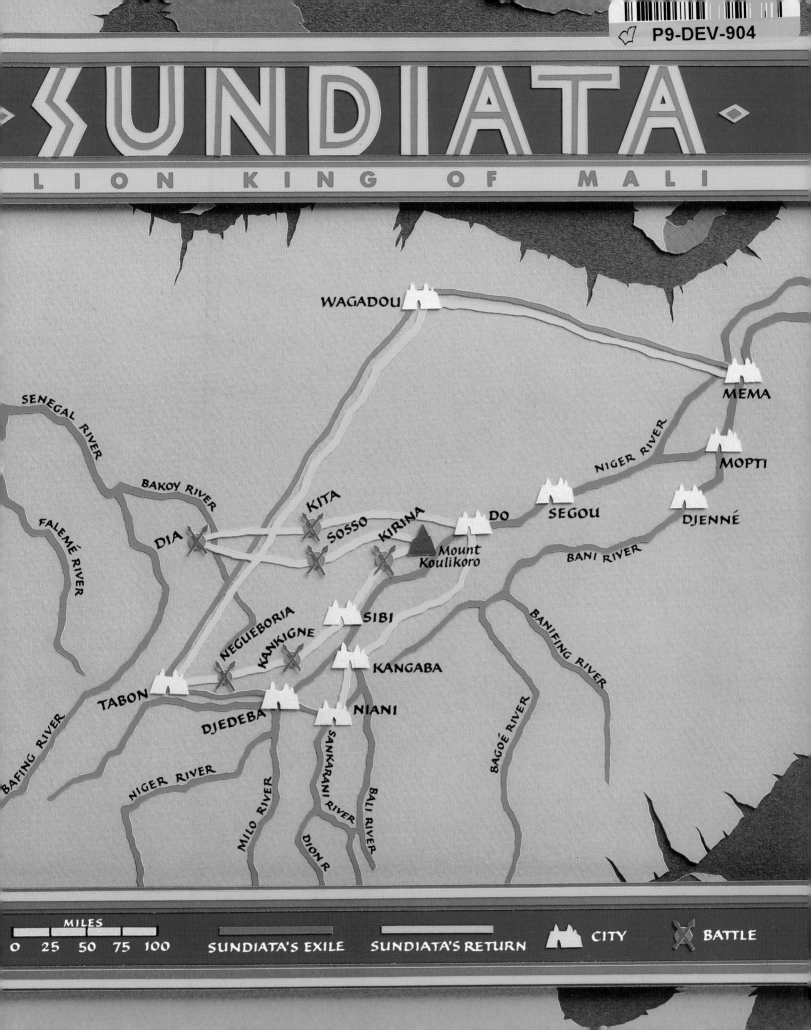

To Gordon and Marie

Clarion Books • a Houghton Mifflin Harcourt Publishing Company imprint • 3 Park Avenue, 19th Floor, New York, New York 10016 • Text and illustrations copyright © 1992 by David Wisniewski. • All rights reserved. For information about permission to reproduce selections from this book, write to trade. permissions@hmhco.com or to Permissions, Houghton Mifflin Harcourt Publishing Company, 3 Park Avenue, 19th Floor, New York, New York 10016. Printed in China. Library of Congress Cataloging-in-Publication Data Wisniewski, David. Sundiata: lion king of Mali / David Wisniewski. p. cm. Summary: The story of Sundiata, who overcame physical handicaps, social disgrace, and strong opposition to rule Mali in the thirteenth century. ISBN 0-395-61302-7 PA ISBN 0-395-76481-5. 1. Keita, Soundiata, d. 1255—Juvenile Literature. 2. Mandingo (African people)—Biography—Juvenile Literature. 3. Mandingo (African people)—Kings and rulers—Juvenile Literature. [1. Keita, Soundiata, d. 1255. 2. Kings, queens, rulers, etc. 3. Mandingo (African people)—Biography. 4. Blacks—Biography. 5. Mali—History.] I. Title. DT533.K45W57 1992 91-27951 966.23'01'092—dc20 [B] CIP AC SCP 28 27 26 Map calligraphy by Jeanyee Wong
4500745217

Photography of cut-paper illustrations by Lee Salsbery

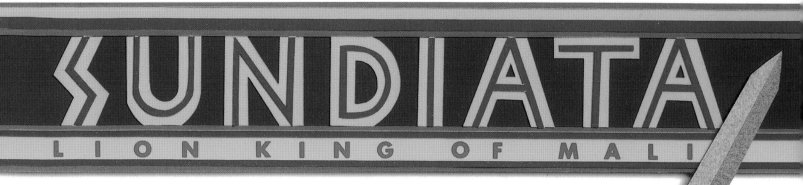

SUNDIATA
LION KING OF MALI

Story and Pictures by DAVID WISNIEWSKI

Clarion Books · New York

Listen to me, children of the Bright Country, and hear the great deeds of ages past. The words I speak are those of my father and his father before him, pure and full of truth. For we are *griots*. Centuries of law and learning reside within our minds. Thus we serve kings

with the wisdom of history, bringing to life the lessons of the past so that the future may flourish.

Listen, then, to the story of Sundiata, the Lion King, who overcame all

As the lion rules the savannah, with power and grace, so did Maghan Kon Fatta rule Mali. One day two hunters approached his throne. Between them walked a maiden, hunchbacked and ill-favored. King Maghan caught his breath, for such a visit had been foretold.

"Great King," said the hunters, "we come from the land of Do, where a terrible buffalo ravaged the countryside. We slew it, and in gratitude the king of Do bade us bring this damsel to you. Her name is Sogolon Kedjou. Though homely, she is said to possess the very spirit of that buffalo, strong and courageous."

"Of such spirits great kings are born," whispered Maghan's *griot*. "The son of lion and buffalo will be mighty indeed!"

So advised, the king wed Sogolon and grew to love her.

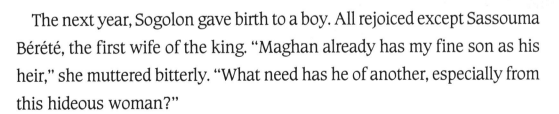

The next year, Sogolon gave birth to a boy. All rejoiced except Sassouma Bérété, the first wife of the king. "Maghan already has my fine son as his heir," she muttered bitterly. "What need has he of another, especially from this hideous woman?"

But the new prince, Sundiata, though blessed by the spirits of buffalo and lion, proved unable to speak or walk. At this, Sassouma Bérété rejoiced.

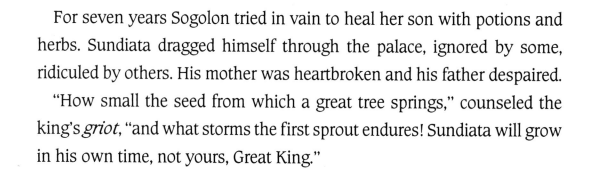

For seven years Sogolon tried in vain to heal her son with potions and herbs. Sundiata dragged himself through the palace, ignored by some, ridiculed by others. His mother was heartbroken and his father despaired.

"How small the seed from which a great tree springs," counseled the king's *griot*, "and what storms the first sprout endures! Sundiata will grow in his own time, not yours, Great King."

The next day Maghan ordered his son brought before him. "My time grows short, Sundiata," he said, "so now I must present the gift that each king gives his heir."

A young man stepped forward. "This is Balla Fasséké," the king continued. "As his father has been my *griot*, so will he be yours. From him

you will learn the history of your ancestors and the laws of this life. May your destiny be fulfilled, my son."

Sundiata sat up slowly, motioned Balla Fasséké to his side, and spoke his first words: "Balla, you are my *griot*."

Maghan's doubts disappeared, and he prepared Sundiata to rule.

But when Maghan Kon Fatta died, the council of elders paid no attention to his wishes. Instead, they allowed the son of Sassouma Bérété to ascend the throne.

Filled with pride, Sassouma lost no time in taunting Sundiata's mother: "It would seem that a walking boy is better than a crawling lion."

Seeing Sogolon's tears, Sundiata summoned Balla Fasséké. "Go to the master smith," he ordered, "and fetch me an iron rod!"

When Balla returned, Sundiata seized the rod with both hands, thrust it into the ground, and raised himself to his knees. Then, with a mighty effort, he pulled himself to his feet. The iron rod fell away, bent with strain, and Sundiata stood alone.

A crowd gathered in amazement as Sundiata took a step, then another and another. "Make way! Make way!" cried Balla Fasséké. "The lion is walking!"

When Sassouma Bérété heard of Sundiata's new strength, she feared he would challenge her son for the throne. Late one night, she called the nine great witches of Mali to her bedside. "You must use your powers to kill Sundiata," she commanded.

"Our magic is useless without his anger," said the witches.

"Go to his mother's garden and pick her spices," hissed Sassouma. "That will surely make him angry enough!"

But when Sundiata found the witches in his mother's garden, he greeted them courteously and helped them gather the spices.

"Alas, queen," the witches reported, "our magic cannot hurt a heart full of kindness. You can do nothing against him."

So Sassouma Bérété bided her time. When Sundiata was ten years old, she had Balla Fasséké sent away to the court of Sosso. This evil land was ruled by Sumanguru, a sorcerer king, whose huge armies and powerful magic were greatly feared. Impressed by the young *griot*'s skill, Sumanguru resolved to keep him in Sosso forever.

Sundiata was angered and saddened by the loss of his friend, and Sogolon's wise words brought new pain. "We must leave Mali," she said, "before our kin fall victim to the queen's hatred. When you are a man, you will return and set all things right." Sundiata reluctantly agreed.

That evening, Sogolon and her children left all that they knew and loved.

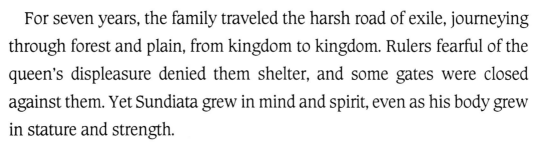

For seven years, the family traveled the harsh road of exile, journeying through forest and plain, from kingdom to kingdom. Rulers fearful of the queen's displeasure denied them shelter, and some gates were closed against them. Yet Sundiata grew in mind and spirit, even as his body grew in stature and strength.

In all these trials, Sundiata never forgot Balla Fasséké. At every court and caravan, he heard of the growing power of Sumanguru and of the unhappy lands under his control.

The family ended their travels in the city of Mema. Weary and ill, Sogolon rested by the banks of the Niger. Sundiata found favor with the king of Mema, who took him on campaigns against the mountain tribes that troubled his kingdom. Observing Sundiata's courage and leadership, he decided to make the young prince his heir. He taught Sundiata the ways of war and government, and looked upon him as a son.

One day, frantic messengers pleaded to speak with Sundiata. "Son of lion and buffalo," they implored, "return to your homeland! Whatever honors you hold in Mema, leave them, and deliver your land from fire and sword."

"What has happened?" asked Sundiata.

"Sumanguru has invaded Mali," they said. "The king and his mother have fled. Our people have taken to the bush to fight, but they are leaderless. We have consulted the seers, and they say that only you can save Mali. The throne of your father awaits you."

"The moment has come, my son," whispered Sogolon. "Your destiny is about to be fulfilled."

Sundiata lost no time. The king of Mema gave him half his army, rank upon rank of armored horsemen carrying great iron spears. Riding at the head of this column, Sundiata stopped at every kingdom that had aided him during his long exile, and gathered more troops. Soon a mighty host covered the savannah, and the thunder of hooves could be heard many miles away.

The two armies clashed on the plain of Kirina. All day the battle raged. Astride his gray charger, Sundiata galloped through the fray, searching for Sumanguru.

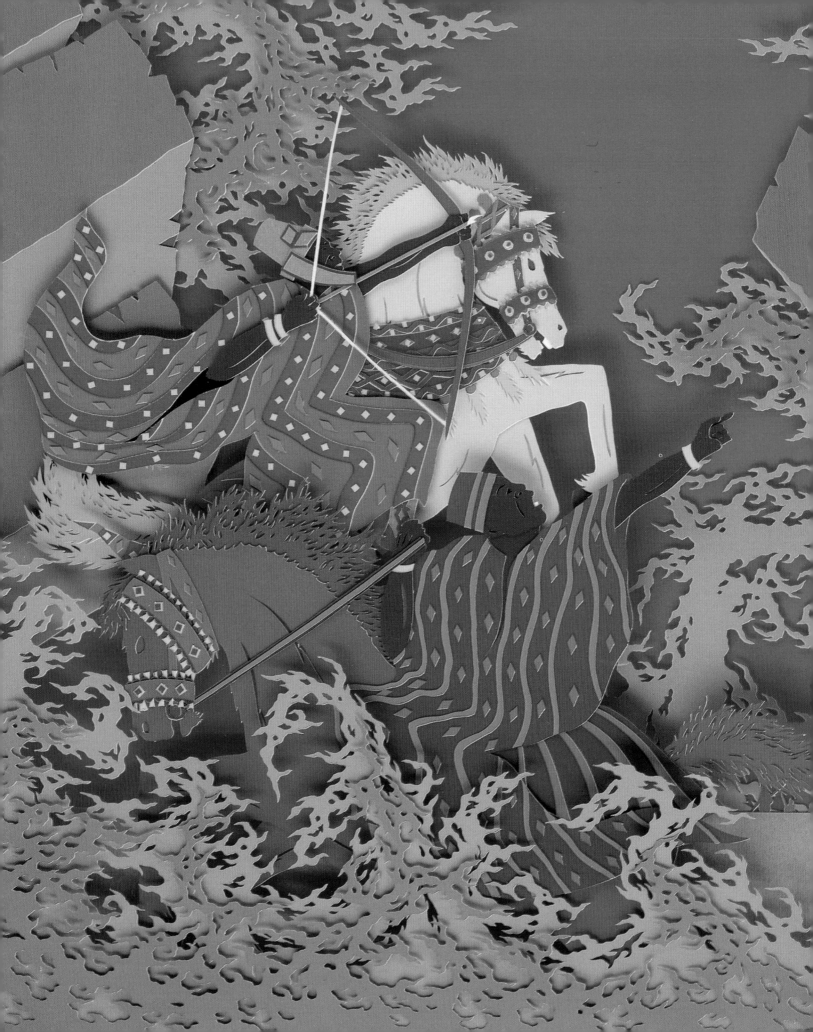

Suddenly, Balla Fasséké was at Sundiata's side. The two friends embraced. "I escaped from the palace and followed Sumanguru's army, hoping to find you," said Balla. "For these seven years I have pretended allegiance to the sorcerer, and I have managed to discover his weakness." He pulled a wooden arrow from his robe. It was tipped with the spur of a white rooster. "This is the *tana* of Sumanguru," Balla continued, "the charm he believes will erase his power. The slightest touch will defeat him utterly!"

Sundiata took the arrow and spurred his horse back into battle. He made his way through the dust and confusion to the hill where the sorcerer stood. Notching the arrow, he drew his mighty bow and let it fly.

The arrow flew straight and true, cutting through Sumanguru's cape and grazing his shoulder. At the sight of the *tana*, the sorcerer let out a harsh cry and galloped from the field.

Pursued by Sundiata and Balla Fasséké, Sumanguru fled to the slopes of Mount Koulikoro and staggered into a dark cave. "Powers of night," he cried, "do not let me fall into the hands of Sundiata!"

It is said that Sumanguru then became one with the stone of the cave, for he was never seen again. Disheartened by his flight, the sorcerer's army went down to defeat.

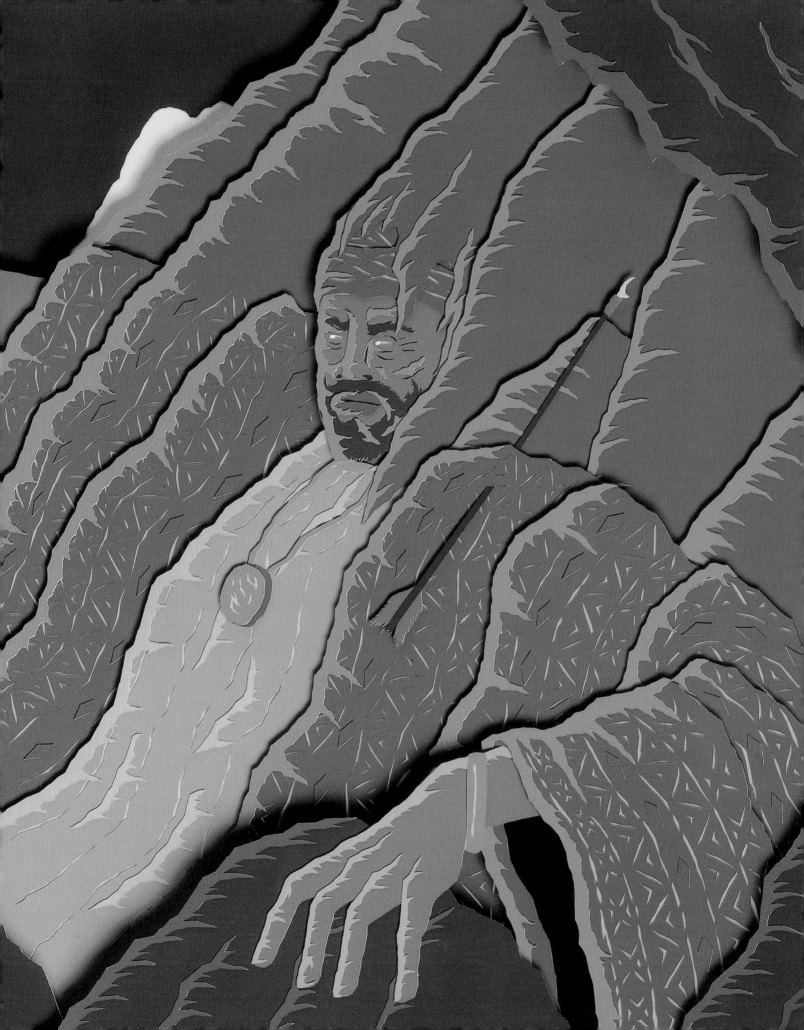

Sundiata returned in glory to Mali. Crowds lined the road the entire journey, shouting his praise. The twelve kings who had aided him in exile and in battle waited at his throne. As Sundiata sat, they drove their spears into the ground before him, swearing allegiance forever.

Sundiata spoke softly and Balla Fasséké conveyed his words to the multitude. "Hatred drove me from this land," he said, "because of what I seemed to be: a crawling child, unworthy of respect and unfit to rule. Mali has suffered great hardship as a result.

"Now I return as your king. Henceforth, none shall interfere with another's destiny. You, your children, and your children's children shall find their appointed place within this land forever."

This came to pass, and Sundiata, the Lion King, ruled the Bright Country for many golden years.

A Note

Around the year 300, the small Soninke chiefdoms between the Niger and Senegal rivers gradually merged, forming the first great empire of West Africa. For the next seven hundred years, the empire of Ghana thrived on brisk traffic in gold, salt, and slaves along Saharan trade routes. Then in 1076 Ghana was invaded by the Almoravids, Islamic Berbers who coveted its riches. Although this force was eventually driven back, the empire was greatly weakened. The small kingdom of Sosso rebelled and gained control of Ghana by 1200.

When Sumanguru came to power in Sosso, he sought to dominate the Malinke kingdom of Mali. Some histories claim that he murdered eleven royal princes of the Keita family, leaving only the insignificant Sundiata unharmed. As subsequent events proved, Sumanguru made a fatal mistake.

Sundiata's journey into exile and back to triumph can be traced on the map at the beginning of this book. He left his father's capital of Niani, only to meet with treachery at Djedeba and cool disregard at Tabon. He traveled by caravan to the trading center of Wagadou and continued on to Mema, where the king took the young prince under his wing. Upon receiving word that Sumanguru had attacked Mali, the eighteen-year-old Sundiata commandeered half of Mema's army and gathered additional troops at Wagadou.

Sundiata's first encounter with the Sosso army was just outside Tabon. A quick victory allowed him to link up with Tabon forces and defeat Sosso again at Negueboria. After turning back a night attack by Sumanguru's troops at Kankigne, Sundiata and his army rested at Sibi and celebrated their victories. The decisive battle took place at Kirina. (The only house left intact from that conflict of 1235 still stands. Designated a shrine, or *Kaba-blon*, by the Keita clan, it is carefully repaired and reroofed every seven years.)

After Sumanguru's death at Mount Koulikoro, Sundiata destroyed Sosso and the allied cities of Dia and Kita. With all fighting now ended, he visited Do to show respect to his mother, who had died in Mema. Then, following a great festivity and coronation in Kangaba, Sundiata made his way back to Niani, the city he had been forced to leave just seven years before.

From this point on, Mali flourished. By the 1300s, Mali's territory encompassed present-day Gambia, Guinea, Mali, Senegal, and portions of Burkina Faso, Mauritania, and Niger. Its principal city of Timbuktu became a renowned center of learning, boasting three universities. Merchants in Timbuktu made their greatest profits from the sale of books. This glorious period was presided over by Mansa Musa, a ruler of great political skill and enormous wealth. (It is noted that during his pilgrimage to Mecca he distributed so much gold in Cairo that the currency there was devalued for twelve years after his visit!) Unfortunately, his successors lacked his power and vision. By 1500 most of Mali had been conquered by Songhai, the third and final great empire of West Africa.

The story of Sundiata has reached modern ears through the unbroken oral tradition provided by *griots* (GREE-ohs). Many African ethnic groups rely on the prodigious memories of these people, rather than written accounts, to preserve the history and wisdom of the past. This version of the Sundiata epic is distilled from the words of Djeli Mamoudou Kouyate, a griot of the Keita clan, in *Sundiata: An Epic of Old Mali*, a compilation written by Djibril Tamsir Niane and translated from the original Malinke by G. D. Pickett (London, 1965).

I have tried to make the illustrations as accurate as possible. The library of the Smithsonian Institution's National Museum of African Art was a great help in this regard. I wish to thank Patrick McNaughton, Ph.D., Associate Professor of African Art at Indiana State University, for reviewing the sketches and offering valuable insights into the history and culture of the Malinke. For example, I had sketched some of the characters with faces and body postures reflecting great emotion. Professor McNaughton pointed out that the Malinke place great value on personal dignity and physical self-control, even in times of severe distress. I redrew the figures with more reserve.

At times, artistic license came into play, generally when documentation was unavailable. For instance, although it is known that battle pennants existed in thirteenth-century Africa, there is little information about what they looked like. The banner on the title page combines authentic Mande spearheads with a design including Malinke fabric motifs; the appliqued lion is based on work by the Fon people from the neighboring country of Benin. In some cases I have used pottery and textile patterns for architectural detailing. And I have shown the nine great witches of Mali in the cotton headwrap, or *chéche*, worn by the desert-dwelling Tuaregs of northern Mali to protect the nose and mouth from blowing sand. Malinke witches would have dressed no differently from the rest of the community, possibly wearing the voluminous robes or *boubou* common to the area, but I chose to depict them in this "foreign" costume to create a heightened sense of mystery and fear.

After the sketches were approved by the editor, I prepared a tracing paper rendition, as detailed as possible. Then, using carbon paper, I transferred the elements of the illustration to the back of the colored papers used in the final art. Each detail was cut out with a #11 X-Acto blade. The pieces were assembled with double-stick photo mountings and foam tape. Finally, the completed pieces were photographed, with light and shadow controlled to capture the most dramatic effect.